THE MIND–BODY PROBLEM

The Mind–Body Problem

An Opinionated Introduction

D. M. Armstrong
UNIVERSITY OF SYDNEY

Westview Press
A Member of the Perseus Books Group

Focus Series

Copyright © 1999 by Westview Press, A Member of the Perseus Books Group

Published in 1999 in the United States of America by Westview Press, 5500 Central Avenue, Boulder, Colorado 80301–2877, and in the United Kingdom by Westview Press, 12 Hid's Copse Road, Cumnor Hill, Oxford OX2 9JJ

Library of Congress Cataloging-in-Publication Data
Armstrong, D. M. (David Malet), 1926–
   The mind–body problem : an opinionated introduction / D. M. Armstrong
     p. cm.
   Includes bibliographical references and index.
   ISBN 0-8133-9056-7 (hardcover).—ISBN 0-8133-9057-5 (pbk.)
   1. Philosophy of mind.   2. Mind and body.   I. Title.
BD418.3.A75   1999
128' .2—dc21   99-19443
                                                        CIP

10   9   8   7   6   5   4   3   2   1

For Bill and Mary

CONTENTS

TABLES AND FIGURES

PREFACE

This book is based on lectures on the philosophy of mind that I have given and developed over many years, at Sydney University, at the University of California at Irvine, at Franklin and Marshall College, and most recently at Yale University. The questions and comments of students have been a continuous stimulus.

I thank Peter Anstey for scholarly assistance; Keith Lehrer for swiftly taking up my tentative idea of making an introductory book out of the lectures so that, in a moment, I had a contract on my desk; Sarah Warner, my acquisitions editor; David Toole for his magnificent copyediting; Kim Sterelny, who kindly read the whole manuscript and made many valuable suggestions; and the anonymous referees for Westview Press. But above all I would like to thank Bill Lycan, whose thinking about the mind, together with his friendship, has meant so much to me over the years. I dedicate the book to him and his wife, Mary.

D. M. Armstrong
University of Sydney

CHAPTER ONE

Introduction

This chapter does three things. First (1.1), it sets out the general principles that I have tried to observe in writing the book. Second (1.2), it gives a brief summary of each further chapter. Third (1.3), it makes a suggestion, based on my own practice, to anybody who considers using the book as the basis for lectures and examinations.

1.1. General principles

The mind–body problem is the problem of what the mind is, what the body is, and, especially, what relation they stand in to each other. This book is based upon lectures that I gave for many years at Sydney University. It is not intended for students who have not yet done any philosophy. For North American students an introductory philosophy course is a desirable preliminary. For British and Australasian students, it is probably best as a second or third year course.

The book has three further features: It is in some degree *historical;* it is *dialectical;* and it is *opinionated.* Let me explain.

First, though historical, it is not a work of scholarship. It does not pretend to be a history of the mind–body problem. But when we have a problem, either intellectual or practical, it is often immensely valuable to understand something of the history of the problem. How did we get into this mess? It usually gives a better grasp of the tangle to see how it got to be that way, and seeing this is likely to help in solving the problem. And with the mind–body problem we need all the help we can get. Many contemporary texts in the philosophy of mind are so anxious to introduce the student to the very latest ideas and arguments that the wood gets lost in the examination of tree after contemporary tree. An approach that is at least partly historical should help to see the wood again.

So I start with Descartes in the seventeenth century, who set the terms of the debate for nearly three centuries and still influences it today. I go on to David Hume's critique of Descartes in the next century and what may be thought of as Thomas Huxley's development of Hume's position in the nineteenth century. Then we are ready to move to Gilbert Ryle's quasi-Behaviourism in the late 1940s, to the Identity theory of U. T. Place and J.J.C. Smart that began as a critique of Ryle, and then on to the successors to the Identity theory. These successor positions are the ones that are dominant today. But the story of how these positions were reached should make us understand them better.

Second, this more or less historical examination of the problem is dialectical. I mean by this that the emphasis will be on the way that the position of one philosopher, or group of philosophers, developed out of a wrestling with, or an examination of, a position taken earlier. We will be following the story, or a significant part of the story, of the running discussion about the mind–body relation that has gone on among philosophers from Descartes to the present day. The emphasis will be continually on the arguments that were used. I sum this up by saying that the treatment will be dialectical.

Finally, the book will be opinionated. It will argue for a certain point of view, in particular for a Materialist solution to the mind–body problem. I do not do this because I wish to be dogmatic. Philosophy is difficult; the mind–body problem is particularly difficult, and no philosopher (or anybody else) should claim to *know* the truth about this matter. It is also true, though, that without a point of view it seems to be impossible to survey and to organize any illuminating discussion. The attempt to stand above the battle, as attractive as it may sound in theory, does not seem to be helpful. Bias seems to be inevitable in presenting arguments about such a deep and fundamental matter. Indeed, without a point of view, a bias, a philosopher is nothing.

What can we do about bias, then? One thing that we can do is to be up-front and declare our bias. I do this by saying that I lean rather strongly toward a Materialist account of the mental. I see the story as a move from Descartes' spiritualist account of the mind to a much more plausible identification of mind with the physical brain. A second thing that we can try to do about bias is much more difficult. We must search out what we take to be the strongest objections to the position we wish to take, state them as fairly as we can, and answer them as plausibly as we can. Philosophers regularly show their deepest worth not so much in advancing penetrating arguments against opponents (where a lot of the fun is), but rather in appreciating which arguments against their position are the arguments that must be answered, and in producing answers of weight and substance to these arguments.

The last three chapters of the book will be devoted, therefore, to what I take to be the main objections to Materialist theories of the mind. I will consider in turn whether three traditional objections to Materialism—consciousness, the sensible qualities, and the phenomenon that philosophers call 'intentionality'—should make us embrace an anti-Materialism about the mind.

1.2. An overview of later chapters

Now for a quick account of the eleven chapters to come. It may help to orient the reader by laying out the bare bones of the story.

Cartesian Dualism.   I begin, as advertized, with Descartes. He held a two-substance theory. The mind is a spiritual, immaterial, substance. The body is a material substance, working according to physical laws. A human being is some intimate, though rather mysterious, union of the two substances. This sort of theory is now called Cartesian Dualism, after Descartes. (You have to be quite an important person to get your own adjective like this!)

Bundle Dualism.   In subsequent philosophical reflection, after Descartes, both spiritual and material substance came under attack. For our purposes, it is the attack on spiritual substance that is of special importance. The great attack on spiritual substance was that launched by the sceptical Scotsman: David Hume. He accepts Descartes' view that the mental is immaterial. But he dissolves the spiritual substance into what he calls 'a bundle of perceptions'. For Hume, the mind is not a single immaterial thing, as it is for Descartes, but, rather, a bundle of little immaterial things.

Epiphenomenalism. Descartes believes in mind–body inter-action. For him, the body acts on the spiritual substance, and the spiritual substance acts on the body. He concedes that this interaction is mysterious, but says that one cannot deny that it happens. Hume, similarly, accepts interaction between the 'bundle of perceptions' and the body. However, later thinkers became increasingly worried about how this interaction is possible. In particular, they worried about how the immaterial mind could act on the material body.

Suppose, then, that (1) you dissolve the mind into a bundle of non-material phenomena; but (2) you deny that this bundle can act on the body, in particular, you deny that it can act on the brain. You have arrived at the position now known as Epiphenomenalism. This position was put forward in the nineteenth century by Thomas Huxley, best known as the defender of, and propagandist for, Charles Darwin. We will look at Huxley's Epiphenomenalism.

Ryle. Epiphenomenalism is Dualism rather near the end of its tether. Mind and body are still conceived of as two quite different sorts of realm, but the mental realm is both dissolved into a mere bundle of perceptions and, still worse, made causally impotent with respect to the body. The question then arises whether the non-physical mental realm can be swept away altogether. The incredible success of the physical sciences makes the idea of a purely phy-sicalist scheme of things look rather attractive.

In psychology, this drive towards the physical gives rise, in the 1920s, to the Behaviourism of J. B. Watson and others. All there re-ally is to the mind are the physical actions of human beings. In phi-losophy also, various thinkers, in particular Ludwig Wittgenstein, tried to get away from a two-realm view. The most accessible of these philosophers is Gilbert Ryle in his book *The Concept of Mind* (1949). We will examine his position.

The Identity theory. Many philosophers, however, were dis-satisfied with the Behaviourist and Rylean denial of two realms. They argued that when we consider such things as our perceptions and, more generally, consciousness, then we are forced to admit an inner realm of the mental. The question then arose, for scientifically oriented philosophers, how it is possible to reconcile the existence of inner mental phenomena with Materialism. From these two intellectual pressures arose the Identity theory. Perception and consciousness exist—they cannot be dissolved into behaviour—but, the Identity theorists said, they are not processes embodied in a spiritual substance or anything like that. They are simply physical processes in the brain. The Identity theory was put forward by Herbert Feigl, U. T. Place, and J.J.C. Smart. We will look at the now classic, and widely anthologized, articles "Is Consciousness a Brain Process?" (Place, 1956) and "Sensations and Brain Processes" (Smart 1959).

The Causal theory.   Place and Smart continued to go a long way with Ryle. Although putting forward a brain process theory of perceptions and consciousness, they accepted what Ryle had to say about other aspects of the mind. In effect, they remained half-Behaviourists.

Some philosophers, in particular David Lewis and D. M. Armstrong[1], thought that this was an unsatisfactory compromise. If you are prepared to identify perceptions and consciousness with brain processes, then why not go the whole way and identify *all* mental processes, events, and states with brain processes, events, and states? Lewis and Armstrong suggest that we do this by giving a causal analysis of all mental concepts. In Lewis's phrase, the concept of the mental is that which plays a certain causal role. For instance, a purpose to get a beer from the fridge can be seen as an inner cause that, in appropriate conditions, would bring about behaviour that did the job. It is then argued (a second step) that what in fact plays this causal role are physical processes, and such, in the brain.

Eliminativism.   A still more radically Materialist view is put forward by Paul Feyerabend and Richard Rorty. In a way, they agree with anti-Materialists, such as Descartes, about the mind. Our notion of the mental, they think, is indeed the notion of something non-physical. But as convinced physicalists, they then argue: So much the worse for the mental. What contemporary science teaches us, they think, is that there are no minds, nor anything mental at all. There are only physical processes in the brain. Later Eliminitavists, in particular Paul and Patricia Churchland, do not take quite this line. But they agree in thinking that the existence of the mental is a mere folk theory that should be replaced with a neurophysiological account of the workings of the brain.

Functionalism. Functionalism is the more or less prevailing orthodoxy about the mind–body problem among analytic philosophers today. Early figures were Hilary Putnam and Jerry Fodor, and the latter became a sort of high priest of Functionalism. The Causal theory of Lewis and Armstrong can also be accounted a variety of Functionalism. Mental processes, and such, are to be defined in terms of the function they serve, but different ways of spelling out this notion of function are to be found: causal function, evolutionary function, computing function, function as in an organizational flowchart. It is generally assumed, in addition, that the actual entities that carry out the function are material processes in the brain.

Objections to Materialism. Materialist theories of the mind do not have it all their own way in contemporary analytic philosophy. There are three main lines of attack made on Materialism, although they tend to get mixed up with each other and need careful sorting out.

(1) *Consciousness.* The first objection to Materialism is that it cannot account for the consciousness that each one of us has both of the world (which includes our own body) and, still more, of the workings of our own mind. In Chapter 10, I make an attempt to give an account of consciousness that is at least compatible with Materialism.

(2) *The sensible qualities.* We experience the world as involving various qualities. Some of these qualities—for instance, seen colour, heard sound, tastes, smells, felt heat, the different qualities that we associate with our different bodily sensations and mental images, also perhaps the qualities of our emotions—are qualities that are not easy to fit into a scientific worldview. Yet we cannot deny their existence; so again we have reason to think that Materialism is seriously incomplete. This objection seems more difficult for the Materialist to deal with than the objection concerning consciousness. I will make an attempt, nevertheless, to sketch a Materialist account of the sensible qualities.

(3) *Intentionality.* Many, perhaps all, mental processes, events, and states have a property that philosophers, using a term derived

from the medieval philosophers, call 'intentionality'. (It has nothing special to do with intentions, though intentions do have intentionality.) It is the way that mental things point beyond themselves to other things that need not be mental at all, and, amazingly, need not even exist. Suppose that I think of a friend who lives far away. It is him I am thinking of. But how could a mere brain process reach out in this way? I can also think of an imaginary playmate I had as a young child. How can a brain process thus point to what does not even exist? For the Materialist, this is probably the hardest problem of all about the mind. I will argue that we can see the beginnings of an account of intentionality that is compatible with Materialism, but I admit that much work remains to be done.

1.3. A note to instructors

Persons considering using this book in teaching may be interested in my own procedures when giving the lectures on which this book is based. I asked as work for the course one essay, and an examination where three questions had to be answered. The essay was supposed to deal with the main themes of what are now the chapters from Chapter 2 to the end. Which chapter was selected was up to the student. The examination contained just one question, of a simple and direct nature, on each topic. Students could pick any three questions, with the exception of the question that covered the chapter that their essay had dealt with. I advised the students of all this from the beginning. They thus had to come to definite terms with the materials in four of the eleven chapters.

I offer a list of readings and references, sometimes with some comment, at the end of each chapter; they are thus readily available for essays and for preparations for examinations.

Notes

1. I say 'Armstrong' here rather than 'I' to try to be more objective!

Readings and references

Braddon–Mitchell, David, and Frank Jackson. 1996. *Philosophy of Mind and Cognition*. Oxford: Blackwell. This would make a useful companion to the present volume. Its approach is not historical, and it takes up certain matters, such as the use of the methodology of possible worlds in the philosophy of mind, and the theory of reference in semantics, that are not dealt with here. There are useful guides to reading, and a glossary of notions is provided.

Campbell, Keith. 1984. *Body and Mind.* 2d ed. Indiana: University of Notre Dame Press. Perhaps the clearest introduction to the mind–body problem ever written. Although published some years ago, it is still useful today. It is also quite brief. The second edition added a whole new chapter on Functionalism. It has an extensive bibliography.

Kim, Jaegwon. 1996. *Philosophy of Mind.* Boulder, Colo.: Westview Press. Another useful recent introduction that would also make an excellent companion to the present volume.

Lycan, William G. 1990. *Mind and Cognition.* Cambridge, Mass:. Blackwell. A useful book of readings, organized by topic.

Rosenthal, David. 1991.*The Nature of Mind.* New York: Oxford University Press. Another useful book of readings, but with a more historical approach.

CHAPTER TWO

Descartes' Dualism

The interpretation of Descartes accepted here is disputed by a number of scholars. They want to modify the story, at least in some degree. It is, however, the interpretation that has been accepted by the analytic tradition. It is the Descartes presented here that later philosophers who took up the mind–body problem were reacting to. Our purposes here demand no more than this. Those who are interested in alternative interpretations should consult G. Baker and K. Morris, Descartes' Dualism; *and Stephen Gaukroger,* Descartes: An Intellectual Biography.

Descartes holds that mind and body are two quite different sorts of substance. The mind is an immaterial substance. The essential attribute of this sort of substance, meaning by 'essential attribute' the property that it must have on pain of not existing at all, is *consciousness.*[1] The body is a material substance. The essential attribute of this sort of substance, the property that it must have on pain of not existing, is *extension* (spatial dimension). The human person is some sort of union of a mind and a body. Descartes writes:

> Every substance has a principal property that constitutes its essential nature, and all others are reduced to this. Extension in length, breadth, and depth is what constitutes the very nature of corporeal substance; consciousness is what constitutes the very nature of a conscious substance. For any other possible attribute of body presupposes extension, and is, so to say, an aspect of an extended thing; and likewise whatever is found in the mind is merely one aspect or another of consciousness. (*Principles of Philosophy*, pt. I, sec. LIII)

We should note, however, that Descartes holds that above the substances of mind and body there is God, who, strictly speaking, is the only true substance:

> We can mean by substance nothing other than a thing existing in such a manner that it has need of no other thing in order to exist. There can indeed be only one substance conceived as needing *absolutely* [my italics] no other thing in order to exist; namely, God. We can see that all other substances are able to exist only by means of God's co-operation. (*Principles of Philosophy*, pt. 1, sec. LI)

The philosopher Mario Bunge has spoken of Descartes' account of mind and body as an 'ambiguous legacy'. What did he mean by this? The first point is that Descartes' Dualism, his view that the mind and the body are two quite different sorts of things, already makes his legacy ambiguous. Nobody, or at any rate no systematic thinker, really likes a Dualism. It offends against the spirit of intellectual economy. How much better if we can find a single set of principles that can explain all the phenomena. So it is not surprising that in later philosophizing influenced by Descartes you find attempts (1) to have mind swallow up matter (this is Idealism—a different sense of the word from having high ideals!); (2) to have matter swallow up mind (Materialism—nothing to do with being 'materialistic' in matters of everyday life!).

But second, Descartes was like a fairy godmother to each of his children: the immaterial substance that is mind and the material substance that is body. Fairy godmothers traditionally appear at your cradle and give you a gift to help you for the rest of your life. Descartes gave a gift to both sorts of substance, a gift to mind and a gift to body. Those who went towards Idealism were persuaded by the gift given to mind, those who leant towards Materialism were persuaded by the gift given to body.

To the mind Descartes gave epistemological advantage. In Descartes' thought the mind is first and best known. This doctrine won widespread acceptance and is one of the major reasons why Western philosophy tended for a long time to lean toward the Idealist side. Instances of Idealism are found in Leibniz and Berkeley, in many of the most influential passages in the writings of Hume, in Kant and Hegel, and in England's F. H. Bradley. The tradition faltered only in the twentieth century; Idealism is now a minority view.

Descartes' theory of the material world had its weaknesses, and much of its detail was overthrown by Isaac Newton. But Descartes' general mechanist orientation turned out to be progressive, particularly for physiology, and especially for the study of the human body. It was the way ahead. There was a sharp contrast here with the spiritual theory of the mind, which turned out not to be capable of fruitful theoretical development. You could not base much of a psychology on it. Scientifically, the materialist side grew stronger and stronger, and eventually philosophy, or at any rate analytic philosophy, responded to that. (Philosophers take their time in responding!) In the twentieth century the philosophical battle between the Idealists and the Materialists, the battle of the Gods and the Giants as Plato called it in his dialogue *The Sophist*, has largely gone the way of the Materialists.

2.1. Descartes on the body

With respect to the body Descartes is a thoroughgoing materialist or *physicalist*. Such a view is often now taken for granted, especially in scientific circles. But it was by no means taken for granted in Descartes' day. He was something of a pioneer then, one of those who brought about the decisive break with the Aristotelian-medieval tradition of thought about the body. In Chapter 4 we will see the scientific tribute that Thomas Huxley pays him.

For Aristotle, and for the Scholastics, there is a deep division in nature between the organic and the inorganic realms, between living things and mere matter. (A linguistic fossil that records the old distinction is the contrast between 'organic' and 'inorganic' chemistry. But nowadays organic chemistry is no more than the chemistry of carbon.) According to Aristotle organic matter (plants, animals) operates according to quite different and more sophisticated principles from the inorganic. Aristotelians spoke of anything organic as having a 'vegetative soul'.[2] This was not a thing or substance, rather it was an inner principle of operation, one that sets the organic apart from the inorganic. This tradition of thought did linger on among some biologists. In more recent times they called themselves Vitalists. I think the tradition is just about extinct now.

Descartes, by contrast, sees the whole organic realm as only *appearing* to work according to special organic principles, according to special laws. The truth, he thinks, is that organic nature obeys the very same laws of nature as the inorganic realm. The difference is due solely to the special and sophisticated setup in organic things such as trees. As J.J.C. Smart is accustomed to putting it, it is just a matter of the sophistication of the wiring diagram. This was a most important break with the Aristotelian tradition. And it turned out to be the way ahead.

As a result of this break with older thought, Descartes conceives of human bodies as just mechanisms working according to purely physical principles. Our bodies can be acted upon by our immaterial minds, of course. But apart from this, they are just particularly wonderful mechanisms. Descartes was very impressed by machines, especially mechanical statues that mimicked simple human actions like raising an arm. Apparently this was a craze of the time in France!

You might say that, despite his avowed Dualism, Descartes had already put psychology on the defensive. The rest of the natural world (including even the nonhuman animals, as we shall see in Chapter 4, when we discuss Descartes' views on animals) was handed over to physics and to purely physical principles of explanation. For Descartes human minds are the only exceptions in nature to this rule. Descartes is really stacking the cards in favour of Materialism, although it took philosophers, at least, a long time to see the point.

2.1.1. Descartes' rejection of final causes in nature

An important part of Descartes' 'philosophy of the body' is his rejection of 'final causes' in nature. For Aristotle and the Scholastics it is permissible to explain what happens in nature in terms of the end to which that happening tends. The eye exists in order for the beings that have eyes to see. The final cause of the eye is seeing. The acorn exists in order to become an oak. That is the final cause of the acorn. In Aristotle, at least, this end for which a thing exists is not imposed upon a thing from the outside. For instance, it is not just God's purpose for the thing. Instead, it is *immanent*, meaning that it dwells within the thing. The thing (or it could be a process) is naturally, of its own nature, pointed to some end.

Clearly, if there is final causality in nature at all, we can expect to find it in organic things. It is natural enough to postulate final causes to explain the growth and workings of plants and animals. But Descartes completely rejects such *teleological* or final causality in physical explanation. All physical causation is *efficient* causality. It is *a tergo*, from the back, from the past, and not *a fronte,* from the front, from the end sought in the future. God may have had certain purposes in creating material things such as human bodies working according to certain physical laws. But these laws are laws of efficient causality.

2.2. Descartes on the mind

For Descartes the essence of mind is consciousness. Descartes never offers any arguments for this view, and, indeed, as we shall see, the position is not particularly plausible. Amazingly, though, it dominated Western thinking about the mind for the next three centuries. Descartes draws at least three consequences out of this doctrine of the essence of mind, none of which, it seems, is there much reason to accept.

2.2.1. The mind is mentally active at all times

Consciousness is a difficult notion, and one object of this book will be to become a little clearer about it. One thing does seem clear: Consciousness is some sort of *activity*. Suppose that there is a mind, but at a certain time, perhaps as a result of physical injury, there is no mental activity in that mind: no thinking, and no sensation. There cannot then be any consciousness in that mind at that time. We can conclude that consciousness is an activity of the mind.

Descartes then moves from his assumption that consciousness is the very essence of the mind to the conclusion that the mind is conscious at all times that it exists. Given his premiss, his conclusion seems to follow. But the conclusion he draws is strange, which gives us good reason to think that his premiss is false. It leads Descartes to say that infants are conscious, and so mentally active, "even in a mother's womb".[3] He does hasten to add that "this does not mean that I hold the conviction that an infant meditates on metaphysical truths in its mother's womb". Rather, he says, "if one may make any conjecture about this obscure matter, it is thoroughly reasonable to suppose that a mind newly united to an infant body is wholly occupied having confused awareness, or sensation, of such ideas as pain, enjoyment, heat, cold" (from a letter of Descartes).

This conjecture, however, seems to be a typical case of a philosopher forcing the facts to fit in with his *a priori* theory, in this case the view that consciousness is the essence of the mental. Descartes was criticized on this point, in particular by John Locke, who made a famous remark: "Methinks, every drowsy nod shakes their doctrine, who teach, that the soul is always thinking" (*Essay,* bk. II, chap. 1, sec. 13). He could have said 'always conscious' instead of 'always thinking'.

Whether total mental inactivity ever occurs is an empirical question, and not one for a philosopher to lay down the law about. But we can certainly go this far with Locke: There seems to be no contradiction in the idea of a totally stopped mind. What would such a stopped mind contain? For one thing, it could contain beliefs. (Some of these beliefs, some of the true ones, might satisfy the conditions for knowledge.) A belief would appear to be a continuing state of a mind, a state that persists even when we are not currently conscious of having that belief. For if a belief were not such a continuing state, it is hard to see how, from time to time, it could have influence on our thinking and acting. Again, I can surely point to a sleeping person and say truly "that person believes that the earth is round" although the sleeper is currently mentally quite inactive. Beliefs can be causally quiescent in the life of the mind. A good analogy is information lying idle in the memory bank of a computer. The computer may be switched off, but the information is still there. And even if the computer is actually operating, that particular bit of information need be playing no role in current operations.

A stopped mind might also contain long-term, standing, purposes and also practical know how, such as knowing how to tie one's shoelaces. It seems that Descartes should have said only that the essence of mental *activity* is consciousness. That is at least a more defensible position, even if still controversial.

2.2.2. Where there is mental activity, we are always aware of it

But Descartes commits himself to much more than the proposition that there is mental activity going on in the mind at all times. He thinks that we are always *aware* of this mental activity while it is going on. For Descartes there is no *unconscious* mental activity. If mental activity M, occurs in person P, at time T, then, for Descartes, P is aware of M at T. I think he would have argued against somebody who thought there could be unconscious mental activity in a simple way. What is unconscious cannot be conscious, consciousness is the essence of the mental, so mental activity that is unconscious is not possible. Given his starting point—his definition of the mental—it is quite hard to stop him from getting to his conclusion. But the conclusion seems wrong. This should lead us to question his starting point.

The Cartesian tradition here is one of the great sources of resistance in Western thought to the idea that there can be unconscious mental activity and, by extension, unconscious mental states. This was a great source of resistance to the ideas of Freud (whose work is controversial for many other reasons as well, of course); to theories of unconscious perception (sometimes called subliminal perception); to the idea that there is unconscious processing involved in the understanding and manipulating of sentences; and in innumerable other sorts of mental operation. Once again, Descartes is ruling out something—unconscious mental activity—*a priori*, on the basis of a definition of the mental, where he should be inquiring empirically whether unconscious mental activity exists.

Leibniz criticized Descartes on this point. He argued that to be aware of mental activity is itself a (further) mental activity, and so would require a further awareness of the awareness of the original mental activity and so on, ad infinitum. That is impossible, Leibniz says: "It must be that I stop reflecting on all these reflections, and that eventually some thought is allowed to occur without being thought about" (*New Essays*, p. 118). I think this is a strong argument against Descartes' position.

In contemporary philosophy of mind, this doctrine—that if something is in one's mind at T (or at least it is an activity in one's mind at T), then one is further *aware* at T that this something is in one's mind—is called the doctrine of *self-intimation*. The term is due to Gilbert Ryle. Mental entities, or at least mental activities, automatically intimate themselves to their possessors. They are self-luminous. The view has been extraordinarily influential, though Leibniz did hold out against it. I do not think that there is any rea-

son to think that it is true, and there are good reasons, including
Leibniz's argument just given, plus a great deal of empirical psychological evidence, to think it false. (For further criticism, see my *A
Materialist Theory of the Mind*, chap. 6, sec. XI; and my debate-
book with Norman Malcolm, *Consciousness and Causality*, pp.
121–135.) A philosopher who still defends a view that is quite close
to Descartes' view is John Searle. He holds that if a state is mental,
then, necessarily, it must at least be possible for that state to be *accessible* to consciousness. (See his book, *The Rediscovery of the
Mind*, p. 152).

2.2.3. Our awareness of mental activity cannot be wrong

Descartes goes still further. He holds not only that we are aware of
everything currently going on in our mind, but also that this awareness never extends beyond what is currently going on in our mind.
The point is a little bit subtle. Suppose everything going on in the
mind reveals itself to current consciousness. That would be logically
compatible with having in addition (false) awarenesses of items, or
properties of items, that are not there. Descartes, however, also rules
out any false awarenesses. Current consciousness of what is going in
the mind is infallible. (I wonder if Descartes ran the two notions together, thinking that if you had self-intimation you also automatically had infallibility?)

That Descartes subscribes to the infallibility of consciousness is
made clear in the *Second Meditation*. There he says that the all-powerful Deceitful Demon would be able to deceive him into thinking
that he, Descartes, was sitting in front of a hot fire. But that he
seems to see a fire, that he is having visual perceptions as of sitting in
front of a hot fire, that he seems to feel heat, that he is having sensations of heat, about these things, he says, the Demon cannot deceive
him. Nor can he be deceived in any other judgment that confines itself precisely to what is (currently) happening in his own mind.

So everything currently going on in the mind is available to consciousness. And anything that seems to consciousness to be currently going on in the mind is going on there. We can put these two
doctrines of self-intimation and infallibility together and call the result the doctrine of *the perfectly transparent mind*. The mind at any
moment is transparent to itself at that moment. All the goods are in

the shop window, and there never seems to be anything in the shop window that is not there. At this point we can see what it means to say that Descartes gave the mind epistemological advantage over the body, making it first and best known. This position, as noted earlier, gave aid and comfort to Idealist opponents of Materialism.

For myself, I see no reason to accept the doctrine of infallibility any more than self-intimation. Indeed, once you have rejected self-intimation, it is rather implausible to hang on to infallibility. But for reasons of space I will not discuss the matter here. (For detailed criticism, see my *A Materialist Theory of the Mind*, chap. 6, sec. 10; and *Consciousness and Causality*, pp. 135–137.)

The doctrine of the perfectly transparent mind has been extraordinarily influential. As we shall see, it influenced Hume, among others. He sums it up in a remarkable passage: "Since all actions and sensations of the mind are known to us by consciousness they must necessarily appear in every particular what they are [this is self-intimation], and be what they appear [this is infallibility]" (*Treatise of Human Nature*, bk. 1, pt. IV, sec. II.).

I believe that the doctrine of the perfectly transparent mind has been a great disaster for the philosophy of mind, a disaster from which we are only now recovering. I would like to recommend instead the view that everything there is, including our own mind, is an epistemological iceberg. It is true of anything at all that there is much about it that we are not aware of (the iceberg below the waterline). And such awareness as we do have, though often correct, is never logically free from error.

So, summing up this discussion, there are three *anti*-Cartesian propositions about the mind that we should accept:

1. There can be mental states that do not involve mental activity (beliefs, etc.).
2. There can be current mental activity (and mental states) of which the person is unaware.
3. Awareness of our own current mental activity (and mental states) can be mistaken.

It should be noticed, though, that there seems to be no necessary connection between Descartes' view that the essence of mind is consciousness and his view that the mind is an immaterial substance. As

far as I can see, a Cartesian Dualist can abandon the 'perfectly transparent mind' without prejudice to his or her Dualism.

2.3. Descartes on the relation of mind to body

Descartes is an *interactionist*. Body acts on mind. A blow on the
hand causes pain. Mind acts on body. A desire to drink is the cause
of various bodily acts ending with drinking. Two-way causal traffic
between body and mind seems obvious commonsense, the obvious
deliverance of experience. To that extent Descartes' account of the
mind–body relation is satisfactory. But his Dualist theory makes it
difficult for him to give a plausible account of interaction. Given his
starting point, the *how* of the interaction becomes obscure.

Since the spiritual substance that constitutes the mind is immaterial, it is not extended and is not in space as the body is. The mind is
therefore not in contact with the body. But Descartes is keen to emphasize how intimate is the union between the two substances. In a
famous passage in the *Sixth Meditation* he says: "Nature also teaches
by these sensations of pain, hunger, thirst, etc., that I am not present
in my body merely as a pilot in a ship; I am most tightly bound to it,
and as it were mixed up with it, so that I and it form a unit" (par. 13).

This passage does credit to Descartes' eye for the facts. But it is
not clear how his eye for the facts is to be reconciled with his theory
of what a mind is. After all, it seems that Descartes ought to think
that there is a respect in which the pilot is more closely united to the
ship than is the spiritual substance to the body: The pilot is actually
within the ship. The unity of mind and body for Descartes can be
no more than an exceedingly close causal unity.

Suppose that I go to move my arm. Something happens in the
spiritual substance: a volition, an act of will, directed towards moving my arm. As an immediate result of this, something must happen
in the body, presumably in the brain. This happening, via a cascading chain of causes in the body, eventually affects the correct muscles, and the arm moves. Suppose instead that I am hit on the hand.
A cascading chain of causes goes up to the brain, and eventually
there is a critical happening in the brain. As a result of this brain
event, something happens in the spiritual substance: an awareness
that the hand has just been struck. Mind–body unity consists of innumerable two-way causal links of this sort, and nothing more.

This scheme involves difficulties. (1) Where in the brain do these first physical effects on the way down, and these last physical effects on the way up, occur? Descartes, who added anatomy and dissection to all his other scientific interests, suggested the pineal gland because it lay at the centre of the brain. It was an ingenious suggestion, but it can be disproved empirically. The gland can even be excised without affecting mental functioning. The neurophysiologist Sir John Eccles, who is a Dualist, suggests other locations: points where the firing or inhibition of neurons might occur as a result of small changes in electrical charge. His idea is that these changes in charge could be the direct effects, and direct causes, of happenings in the mental substance. (See his book *The Neurophysiological Basis of Mind*, chap. 8, "The Mind-Brain Problem".) The point here is that the Dualist is in rather urgent need of some such scientific theory, preferably one that can be experimentally tested.

(2) There is a particular difficulty about the mind to body link. When the happening in the mind causes the happening in the brain, then the physical system of the brain, its body, and the surrounding environment is broken into and in some degree changed. The physical system develops in a way that it would not have developed if the happening in the mind had not occurred. If the decision to raise the arm is a critical one—say, the general giving the signal to begin the battle—the physical effects might be large. Physical scientists think that physically closed systems conserve energy, that the total energy in the system does not alter. Are we prepared to allow injections of energy into a physical system that remains physically closed?

(3) But the greatest difficulty that most philosophers have felt about the Cartesian theory is the sheer lack of parallel between this sort of causation and any other that we are acquainted with. Here is Princess Elizabeth of Bohemia in correspondence with Descartes:

For the determination of movements seem always to come about from the moving body's being propelled—to depend upon the kind of impulse it gets from what sets it in motion, or again, on the nature and shape of this latter thing's surface. Now the first two conditions involve contact, and the third involves that the impelling thing has extension; but you utterly exclude extension from your notion of soul, and contact seems to me to be incompatible with a thing's being immaterial.

We could not argue now that the only causality that we know anything about is that which involves contact. But it remains true that we still have no clear model for the way that a spiritual happening gives rise to a brain happening, and vice versa.[4] Descartes, in reply, can protest only that the interaction occurs. But that is no reply if what we are trying to assess is the plausibility of his *theory* of that interaction. There cannot be much doubt about the occurrence of mind–body interaction. But there can be doubt about whether this is the interaction of two totally disparate things. A mind–body theory that makes interaction easy and intelligible (as a materialist theory seems to do) is to that extent preferable.

Of course, this is just one place where Dualism does not seem to come off very well. All theories of the mind–body relation get involved in a certain amount of difficulty. The thing that we have to try and judge is what sort of theory seems to come off best *all things considered*. The task is not easy!

2.4. Descartes' arguments for his Dualism

What we will do now is to examine Descartes' two arguments by which he tries to establish his mind–body theory. We look first at his argument from conceivability, and then at his argument from the indivisibility of the mind.

2.4.1. The Conceivability argument

We find this argument in paragraph 15 of the *Sixth Meditation* and also in the *Principles of Philosophy* (pt. I, sec. LX). It is a difficult argument to reconstruct from Descartes' texts, and the commentators are divided about just how it goes. I used to think that it was not a strong argument. But Michael Hooker—in an article to be found in his edited collection, *Descartes: Critical and Interpretive Essays*—has given a rather elaborate reconstruction of the argument that, though it still has difficulties, does make it rather plausible, given Descartes' starting points. Here it is:

> (1) I can conceive of myself existing and no bodies existing. [premiss 1]
> (2) If something is conceivable, then it is possible. [premiss 2]
> So, (3) it is possible that I exist and no bodies exist. [by 1 and 2]

(4) If something is a body, then it is essentially a body. [premiss 3]
So, (5) if I am a body, I am essentially a body. [by 4]
(6) If I am essentially a body, it is not possible that I exist and no bodies exist. [by definition of 'essentially']
So, (7) I am not essentially a body. [by 3 and 6]
So, (8) I am not a body. [by 5 and 7]

I have presented the argument informally, but it is easy enough to rewrite it as a formally valid argument. And premiss 1 looks rather plausible. Descartes can back it up with his famous argument from an all-powerful Deceitful Demon. Surely we can conceive of such a demon, and that this demon should give me the illusion of having a body and living in a material world. It is hard to deny that this is conceivable.

Premiss 2 is much more debatable, and I think that it is in fact false. But let us first consider Descartes' third premiss, that is to say (4). Must a body be essentially a body? It is presumably not necessary, but is just a contingent truth that, say, a certain stone has a certain mass or occupies a certain volume with a certain shape. But is it a necessary truth that it is a *body* (which is what it means to say it is essentially a body)? I don't really know the answer to this, but it is at least a reasonably plausible contention. If (5) is the weakest link in Descartes' argument, then he (or perhaps Hooker?) has given us a quite strong argument for some sort of mind–body Dualism.

But now let us consider the second premiss, the move from conceivability to possibility. This premiss is actually one of the central contentions in Descartes' whole philosophy, and it was in turn accepted by Hume (see the references in Hooker). Furthermore, the Descartes–Hume view became orthodoxy, passing into the Western philosophical tradition. (Descartes himself demands that the conceiving be 'clear and distinct' if we are to make this transition from conceivability to possibility. 'Clear' and 'distinct' are technical terms in his philosophy. Roughly, he means 'fully analyzed'. He argued further that it is not possible for clear and distinct conceptions to be mistaken, which gives him his desired result. This second step is the one we should quarrel with.)

The matter is a little way from the philosophy of mind, but it is so important philosophically that it must be considered. "I can conceive that *p*, so it is at least possible that *p*" is in fact a dubious way of proceeding. Here is a case where the principle seems to break down. For this counterexample to work, you need to accept, as most though not all philosophers accept, that mathematics is a body of necessary truths. Now consider some still unsolved problem in mathematics, for instance Goldbach's conjecture that every even number is the sum of two primes. (A prime number, you will remember, is a number not divisible by any number except itself and the number 1.) Call this conjecture G. Surely we fully understand, and so can clearly and distinctly conceive, both G and not-G. Either the conjecture is true, or else it is not true. Those are the only two alternatives. One of them is a necessary truth, the other is an impossibility, although we do not (at present) know which. We can conceive that G is true, and we can conceive that not-G is true. So we have clearly and distinctly conceived something that is not possible.

A second plausible counterexample: Many contemporary philosophers, following Saul Kripke, argue that it is a necessary truth—though one discovered *a posteriori*, through scientific inquiry—that water is an assemblage of H_2O molecules. Being made up of H_2O molecules is the essence of water. But it is quite easy to conceive that water is not H_2O. So, if Kripke is right, we can conceive something impossible.

This is bad news for the Conceivability argument. Descartes cannot then get to his first conclusion: (3). Let us grant Descartes' premiss (5): If I am essentially a body, it is not possible that I exist and no bodies exist. That entails that if I am a body, then (3) is false. It is not possible that I exist and no bodies exist. It is merely conceivable that I exist and no bodies exist. But we know, from the argument of the two previous paragraphs, that we can conceive the impossible. Maybe this is one of those cases. There is no proof, therefore, that I am not just a body.

Another point, before we leave the argument. Although no commentator I have read mentions the matter, it seems that the Cartesian doctrine of self-intimation could be influencing Descartes' thinking here. For Descartes, we are aware of our own mind and, therefore, aware that we are thinking or conscious beings. But we certainly are not aware that our mind is extended or material. Given this premiss, and given self-intimation, we can conclude that our mind is definitely not extended or material. Must it then not be wholly distinct from our body?

2.4.2. The Indivisibility argument

The second argument (*Sixth Meditation*, par. 23), though not sound as it stands, is again interesting. Furthermore, its structure is perfectly clear. Descartes argues:

(1) The body is a divisible thing.
(2) The mind is an indivisible thing.
So, (3) body and mind are two different things.

The problem lies with the second premiss. It is obviously controversial. Descartes argues: "When I consider the mind—that is, myself, in so far as I am merely a conscious being—I can distinguish no parts within myself." He then goes on to answer an objection: "Nor can the faculties of will, feeling, understanding and so on be called its parts, for it is one and the same mind that wills, feels, and understands."

This reply is not impressive. After all, it is equally one and the same body that has different parts. Descartes seems to be moving illegitimately from the fact that the mind is a *single* thing to the conclusion that it is a *simple* thing. And introspection would seem to go against Descartes here. We can be aware of multiple processes coexisting in our minds. Indeed, Plato argues in the *Republic* (434d–441c) for parts of the soul on the ground that we can entertain inconsistent desires. He gives the example of a man torn between his desire to gaze at corpses lying beside the road and his feeling that this is a shameful desire to indulge.

So the argument is a weak one as it stands. But the general form of the argument is an important one, and, as we shall see, in the hands of philosophers other than Descartes it gives materialists a lot of trouble. The argument uses a principle known to philosophers as the *Indiscernibility of Identicals*. (I apologize for this name!) This principle seems to be necessarily true. If two things, x and y, are identical, then they have exactly the same properties. Or, negatively, which is the important formulation for our purposes, if x and y do *not* have the same properties, then they are *not* identical. In symbols (for those who have some logic):

$$N \ (\forall x)(\forall y)((x = y)) \supset (\forall P)(Px \equiv Py))^5$$

The translation of this is: necessarily, for all objects x and y, if x is identical to y, then, for all properties P, x has P if and only if y has P.

Given this principle, what you have to do is find a property that one of the two things, x or y, has but the other lacks. There are some tricky cases, which we cannot go into here, but they do not affect the present situation. If Descartes is right to say that the body is divisible but the mind is indivisible, then his argument succeeds. But he has made a bad choice of a supposed differentiating property, because it is far from obvious that the mind is indivisible. Indeed, this proposition seems false.

We need a name for this style of argument, and 'Indiscernibility of Identicals' is a bit of an ordeal as a phrase. Let us call it the *Properties argument*. Here is its essence: different properties, so different things. One thing that you must not confuse this principle with is the *Identity of Indiscernibles*, which says: different things, so different properties:

$$N\ (\forall x)(\forall y)(P)((Px \equiv Py) \supset (x = y))$$

This one translates as: necessarily, for all objects x and y, and for all properties P, if x has P if and only if y has P, then x is identical with y. This is a much more controversial principle than the Indiscernibility of Identicals, but fortunately we do not need to discuss it here!

2.5. Mind as a substance

Before leaving Descartes, I will say one thing. I think Descartes was quite right to maintain that the mind is a substance, a unitary thing. The discussion of Hume that we are just about to embark upon will show some of the difficulties in maintaining that the mind is a mere bundle of objects. But that does not necessarily mean that Descartes was right to think that the mind is a spiritual substance. There is at least one alternative: that it is a material substance.

Notes

1. The actual words that Descartes uses are the Latin and the French words for *thought: cogitare* and *penser*, respectively. I follow Elizabeth

Anscombe and Peter Geach (xxxvii n. 2; and the translators note, xlvii–xlviii) in choosing 'consciousness' as the appropriate translation.

2. The Aristotelians of the Middle Ages spoke of the 'vegetative soul' for all organic things; the 'sensitive soul' for all animals; and the 'rational soul' for human beings only.

3. He could have said, as one of my referees has pointed out, that infants have no mind until they are born. But this does not seem a plausible view.

4. It has been suggested that quantum mechanics might provide a model. The so-called collapse of the wave function may be linked with observation, and so perhaps with the mind. But no clear and testable theory seems to have emerged.

5. '$\forall$' translates as 'all'; '=' translates as 'is identical with'; '$\supset$' translates as 'if . . . then'; '$\equiv$' translates as 'if and only if'.

Readings and references for Descartes

Descartes' remarks on the nature of mind, body, and the relation between them are scattered around his writings. A number of passages are usefully brought together in The Nature of Mind, *ed. David M. Rosenthal, New York: Oxford University Press, 1991.*

Anscombe, Elizabeth, and Peter Geach, eds. 1962. *Descartes: Philosophical Writings*. Edinburgh: Thomas Nelson. The 'Letters' section contains the correspondence with Princess Elizabeth.

Armstrong, D. M. 1993. *A Materialist Theory of the Mind*. Paperback ed., with a new preface. London: Routledge.

Armstrong, D. M., and Norman Malcolm. 1984. *Consciousness and Causality*. Oxford: Blackwell.

Baker, G., and K. Morris. 1996. *Descartes' Dualism*. London: Routledge.

Eccles, John. 1953. *The Neurophysiological Basis of Mind*. Oxford: Clarendon Press.

Gaukroger, Stephen. 1995. *Descartes: An Intellectual Biography*. Oxford: Clarendon Press.

Hooker, Michael, ed. 1978. *Descartes: Critical and Interpretive Essays*. Baltimore and London: Johns Hopkins University Press. The essays by Donagan, Hooker, Mattern, Sommers, and Wilson are relevant.

Hume, David. 1739. *A Treatise of Human Nature*. Reprint, ed. L. A. Selby-Bigge. Oxford: Clarendon Press, 1960.

Keeling, S. V. *Descartes*. 1968. Oxford: Oxford University Press. See chapter 5.

Kenny, Anthony. 1968. *Descartes: A Study of His Philosophy*. New York: Random House. See chapter 10.

Leibniz, G. W. 1765. *New Essays on Human Understanding*. Ed. Peter Remnant and Jonathan Bennett. Cambridge: Cambridge University Press, 1981.

Locke, John. 1690–1710. *An Essay Concerning Human Understanding*. Reprint, based on first six editions, ed. P. H. Nidditch. Oxford: Clarendon Press, 1975.

Plato. *The Republic*. See any good edition of Plato's writings.

_____. *The Sophist*. See any good edition of Plato's writings.

Searle, John R. 1992. *The Rediscovery of the Mind*. Cambridge, Mass: MIT Press, A Bradford Book.

Smith, Norman K. 1962. *Studies in the Cartesian Philosophy*. New York: Russell & Russell. See chapter 3, section III.

_____. *Descartes' Philosophical Writings*. 1952. London: Macmillan. See "Letters on the Mind-Body Problem". It contains the correspondence with Princess Elizabeth.

Williams, Bernard. 1978. *Descartes: The Project of Pure Enquiry*. Sussex, England: The Harvester Press. See chapter 10.

Twentieth-century discussion of Dualism

For

Broad, C. D. 1925. *The Mind and Its Place in Nature*. London: Routledge.

Beloff, John. 1962. *The Existence of Mind*. London: Maccgibbon & Kee.

Foster, John. 1991. *The Immaterial Self*. London: Routledge. An important recent defence of Cartesian Dualism.

Against

Armstrong, D. M. 1993. *A Materialist Theory of the Mind*. London: Routledge. See chapter 2, sections II and III.

CHAPTER THREE

Hume's
Bundle Dualism

The text for this section is Hume's Treatise of Human Nature, *bk. 1, pt. IV, sec. V, "Of the immateriality of the soul", and, especially, sec. VI, "Of personal identity".*

We now jump from Descartes in the seventeenth century to Hume in the eighteenth. But we find that the influence of Descartes is still strong. In his philosophy of mind Hume puts forward an empiricist and sceptical version of Cartesian Dualism. Before considering his reduction of the spiritual substance to a bundle of immaterial items, we will look at his defence of Dualism and also of Interactionism.

3.1. Hume's defence of Dualism

Hume argues for mind–body Dualism by using a version of the Properties argument, which we have seen Descartes using. But Hume's version is much more plausible. He says:

> Whatever is extended consists of parts; and whatever consists of parts is divisible, if not in reality, at least in the imagination. But it is impossible anything divisible can be conjoined to a thought or a perception, which is a being altogether inseparable and indivisible. For, supposing such a conjunction, would the indivisible thought exist on the left or on the right hand of this extended divisible body? On the sur-

face or in the middle? On the back or the foreside of it? If it be conjoined with extension, it must exist somewhere within its dimensions.
If it exists within its dimensions, it must either exist in one particular
part; and then that particular part is indivisible, and the perception is
conjoined only with it, not with the extension: or if the thought exists
in every part, it must also be extended, and separable, and divisible, as
well as the body, which is utterly absurd and contradictory. For can
anyone conceive a passion of a yard in length, a foot in breadth, and
an inch in thickness? Thought therefore and extension are qualities
wholly incompatible, and never can incorporate together into one
subject. (*Treatise of Human Nature*, bk.1, pt. IV, sec. V)

Hume, then, is arguing that mental phenomena lack spatial position and spatial extension, and are therefore not material. As more
recent philosophers have put it: It is absurd that a thought should be
located two inches behind the bridge of my nose, or that it should
have a size or a shape inside the brain.

This is a tougher, more plausible, version of the Properties argument that Descartes used to argue for the immateriality of the mind.
It definitely throws the Materialist on the defensive. Can the argument be met? I believe so, although a bit of work is involved. What I
think the materialist should do is first to grant that for many, probably all, mental items, when we introspect, that is when we pay attention to what is currently going on in our own mind, we are not
aware of the spatial nature of the items we attend to. But it is a fallacy, involving an illegitimate shift of the word 'not', to argue from:

(1) We are not aware that mental objects are spatial.
to
(2) We are aware that mental states are non-spatial.

The Materialist should therefore concede (1), deny (2), and up-
hold the spatial nature of the mental as a plausible scientific theory,
though *not* one that is verifiable by introspection.

The first thing to notice is that this suggested reply to Hume's argument would not have impressed Hume himself much. We have already noticed that he takes over the Cartesian doctrine that minds
are perfectly transparent to themselves. So he could argue (strangely
enough, I don't know anywhere that he does): mental objects are

completely self-intimating to introspection; all the goods are in the shop window. If, as you Materialists concede, we are not directly aware of the spatial properties of mental phenomena, then they definitely must lack spatial features.

However, even if we reject the Descartes/Hume view of the mind as completely transparent to itself when it inspects itself, it is still easy to think that the evidence of introspection gives support to the view that the mind is not spatial. Is it not *natural* to pass from the fact that we are not aware by introspection that the mind is spatial (which seems true) to thinking that we are aware that the mind is not spatial?

I think the Materialist can explain this! Consider the Headless Woman Illusion. In this illusion, popular in Victorian times, a woman is presented on a stage completely hung with black. A cloth of the same black is placed over the woman's head. It looks for all the world (I am reliably told) as if the woman lacks a head. Unsophisticated persons might be deceived.

Here we pass from a lack of awareness of the woman's head to the false impression that the woman lacks a head. There is an 'operator shift' from lack of awareness to 'awareness' of a lack. This pattern of reasoning serves us well in most ordinary contexts. If you can't see anybody in the room, then it is likely that there is nobody in the room. The inference only goes wrong in special cases. The Headless Woman case is a deliberately contrived case where the inference does go wrong.

Furthermore, although the inference is utterly natural, it is quite unreliable in many scientific contexts. Most of us now would think that the fact that you cannot perceive molecules, atoms, and fundamental particles is not a good reason for thinking that these things do not exist. They do exist, we think, and are in fact the ultimate constituents that make up the things we perceive. This fact shows us what the Materialist should say in reply to Hume's argument. That our perceptions, sensations, and thoughts are material processes, and so have spatial properties, is a scientific hypothesis that we should not expect to verify by introspection. At the same time, Headless Woman reasoning—the passage from lack of awareness to 'awareness' of a lack—is an utterly natural style of reasoning. So we can actually expect the materialist hypothesis to be *phenomenologically* implausible, even if it is true.

The Materialist also should be able to explain away the appearance of (relative) simplicity in mental phenomena. If Materialism is true, sensations and such are incredibly complex physical phenomena. But we are not introspectively aware of this complexity; so the phenomena give an appearance of simplicity that we find hard to shake off. As Kim Sterelny has pointed out to me, this sort of situation is common in ordinary perception. For instance, we see pictures on a television screen, but we are not able to see the complex structure of little pixels that actually make up the images. We are not perceptually aware of this complexity. The real structure of the pictures does not appear. Perhaps introspective awareness is also like this. Mental phenomena appear to introspection to be far more simple than they really are.

3.2. Mind–body interaction

Like Descartes, Hume accepts mind–body interaction, even though the things that interact are, according to him and Descartes, utterly different and even though their interaction is of a quite unique type. Unlike Descartes, however, Hume does not see this interaction between immaterial mind and material body as any sort of problem. He states what he takes to be the Cartesian worry thus: "Matter and motion, it is commonly said in the schools, however varied, are still matter and motion, and produce only a difference in the position and situation of objects" (bk. 1, pt. IV, sec. V).

Hume rejects this argument, however, on the basis of his notorious 'constant conjunction' or 'regular succession' analysis of causation: the view that 'production' is nothing but a certain sort of thing being regularly followed by a certain sort of thing. He then argues that all objects are susceptible of a constant conjunction, or, as he also puts it, "to consider the matter *a priori*, anything may produce anything". (Note that he is not saying 'anything may produce anything', only that this is so if we consider the matter *a priori*, that is before we have had experience of what is actually followed by what.) "We find, by comparing their ideas, that thought and motion are different from each other, and by experience, that they are constantly united." So, he concludes, we know *a posteriori*, by experience, that immaterial mind and material objects act upon each other.

Actually, Hume didn't need his sceptical analysis of causation as constant conjunction to make his point. All he really needs is the weaker premiss that what causes what is a *contingent* affair, one that is not necessary, one that does not hold 'in all possible worlds'. Most, even if not all, contemporary philosophers would grant Hume this premiss. (I would grant it myself.)

But even granting Hume the assumption that there is no contradiction in the idea of a non-spatial mind and spatial matter interacting, does this concession remove all difficulty? I don't think it does. Consider the point that Princess Elizabeth made against Descartes. Causal connection between the immaterial mind and material body is a quite different form of causal connection from any other that we have experience of, and one whose laws are extremely hard to discern. We might well think that it is a non-conclusive but quite weighty difficulty for Dualism that it has to postulate a special, extra form of causal connection.

3.3. Hume's critique of spiritual substance

Berkeley, who preceded Hume, had attacked the notion of material substance. In particular, Berkeley attacks Locke's rather unattractive theory of substance: substance as an unknowable substratum that supports the properties of material things. For Locke, this substratum is 'something I know not what', which, however, we are forced to postulate because we cannot understand how the properties of things could exist without inhering in something. But Berkeley argues that the Lockean substratum should be swept away and that we should reconcile ourselves to the conception of a material thing as a mere bundle of properties.

Berkeley, however, leaves spiritual substance untouched. Hume may be thought of as widening Berkeley's attack to include spiritual substance. He won't have anything to do with an unknown substratum for the mind any more than for material substance. But Hume's attack is even wider than this. He says:

> There are some philosophers who imagine we are at every moment intimately conscious of what we call our self; that we feel its existence and its continuance in existence; and are certain, beyond the evidence of a demonstration, both of its perfect identity and simplicity.

Hume, however, declares that he can observe no such thing:

> For my part, when I enter most intimately into what I call myself, I
> always stumble on some particular perception or other, of heat or
> cold, light or shade, love or hatred, pain or pleasure. I never can catch
> myself at any time without a perception, and never can observe any-
> thing but the perception.

Persons, he says:

> are nothing but a bundle or collection of different perceptions, which
> succeed each other with an inconceivable rapidity and are in a perpet-
> ual flux and movement. . . . The mind is a kind of theatre, where sev-
> eral perceptions successively make their appearance; pass, repass, glide
> away, and mingle in an infinite variety of postures and situations.
> . . . The comparison of the theatre must not mislead us. They are the
> successive perceptions only, that constitute the mind; nor have we the
> most distant notion of the place where these scenes are represented, or
> of the materials of which it is composed. (bk. 1, pt. IV, sec. VI)

This famous, indeed notorious, account of the mind as a 'bundle of
perceptions' is very much open to criticism. We will look at three
problems that Hume has to face, problems that he seems to have little hope of solving.

3.3.1. Is the mind just mental activity?

One thing is quite clear: Hume accepts the Cartesian identification
of the mind with consciousness; as a result he has to hold, just like
Descartes, that the mind is always active:

> When my perceptions are removed for any time, as by sound sleep,
> so long am I insensible of myself, and may truly be said not to exist.
> And were all my perceptions removed by death, and could I neither
> think, nor feel, nor see, nor love, nor hate after the dissolution of my
> body, I should be entirely annihilated. (bk. 1, pt. IV, sec. VI)

Hume has got himself into the same trouble as Descartes (by following him) but is trying to back out a different way. See Table 3.1.
Both positions are paradoxical. But Hume's position seems even

TABLE 3.1   One Problem, Two Strange Solutions

Descartes and Hume both assert No mental activity → no mind	

So *Descartes* says:
  There is always mental activity
  even in sound sleep, the womb,
  and so on.
	So *Hume* says:
	  In sound sleep, the womb,
	  and so on, we do not exist.

weirder than Descartes'. Is it really true that, as a result of a period of unconsciousness, our mind pops in and out of existence? Does not a soundly sleeping person continue to have beliefs, skills, likes, dislikes, continuing purposes? These things are not active at that time, are not contributing to 'the life of the mind'. But they do not cease to exist. And if they exist at that time, the mind exists at that time.

Hume compares the mind to 'a kind of theatre', but then immediately takes it back, saying that we have no idea of a continuing structure within which the 'perceptions' appear. But we seem to require such a theatre. Does it matter that we can't observe the theatre? It would matter to one who accepted the dogma of a mind perfectly transparent to its inspection of itself. But why accept such a dogma?

3.3.2. Are Hume's 'perceptions' substances?

Hume denies the existence of substance in the Lockean sense of an unknown substratum that supports properties. But there is another conception of substance at work in his thought that he does accept. It is a conception that goes back at least to Aristotle, and that we have already met with in Descartes. It is the conception of 'something which may exist by itself' (Hume's phrase), something that is logically capable of independent existence, or that is, to use another of Hume's phrases, 'a distinct existence'. It takes us to the heart of any systematic philosophy to ask the question: What does this philosophy take the substance(s) of the world to be, in this special sense of the word?

Hume holds (1) that the mental and the physical are distinct and do not overlap; and (2) that the mental is nothing but bundles of 'perceptions'. He is therefore driven to say that each distinct perception is a distinct existence, that is, a distinct substance. Hume's 'perceptions' are similar to what later philosophers called 'sense-data'. A. J. Ayer

rather neatly and wittily called sense-data 'junior substances'. The
same description could be applied to Hume's 'perceptions'.

I don't think we can fault Hume's reasoning here, given his premisses. But it seems that there must be some mistake in at least one of
his premisses, because this doctrine that he has arrived at, that each
distinct 'perception' is a distinct existence, seems false. The point is
that if each perception really is a distinct existence, then it must be at
least logically possible, non-self-contradictory, that the perception
could have existed in independence of the bundle, or indeed in independence of anything else at all.

But is this possible? Here are some of the things that Hume
would count as 'perceptions':

- a sensation of pain
- a feeling of gloom
- a visual impression of something blue
- a thought that it is getting too hot in the room

Could any of these things possibly exist in independence of anything else? I do not have any further argument to back up my view
here, but I suggest that Hume has followed out his argument to
reach a conclusion that is wrong.

It looks to me as if Hume has misconstrued the nature of his 'perceptions', his mental 'objects'. They are not things capable of independent existence. Instead, they are like, say, a grin or a motion. No
grin without something further: a face that grins. No motion without something further: something that moves. A natural way to go
is to say that sensations, feelings, perceptions, thoughts, and so on
are not things but *states* of a thing, some sort of attribute or property of a thing. What thing? The mind, of course. The thing that
Hume denies.

Hume, no doubt, would raise the difficulty that we are quite unable to perceive this thing of which it is alleged that the pains and
such are states. And if, as he does, we think that the mind is transparent to itself, then this is a great difficulty. But if we discard this
Cartesian dogma, then the way is open to see the mind as something
postulated, or reasoned to, rather than as something observed.

The mind, even our own mind, becomes a (primitive) theoretical
concept. We are aware of mental goings on in ourselves. These go-

ings on seem not to be the sort of things that are capable of independent existence. So we are forced to postulate something in which they inhere, in which they are states or processes. What the concrete nature of that substance is, is a matter for further speculation. A Cartesian will think it is a spiritual substance. A Materialist will think it is the physical brain.

3.3.3. Hume's problem of unifying the bundle

Minds do not, as far as we know, overlap. If, as Hume does, you break up the mind into a bundle of 'perceptions', then, considering all the perceptions going on in the world at the same time, you need to separate them into non-overlapping bundles. But then you need some principle, some 'unity relation', that will yield these non-overlapping bundles. Hume is well aware of the problem. In Section VI Hume claims to solve the difficulty. But in the famous Appendix to the *Treatise*, he says that the problem is too hard for him. In later philosophical discussion this problem was discussed extensively.

Hume thinks of the problem as the problem of securing the identity of the bundle over time, the problem of saying what makes your perceptions yesterday part of the same bundle as your perceptions today, and not part of the same bundle as my perceptions yesterday and today. This can be called the problem of *diachronic* unity, unity over time. But there is a further problem that Hume does not consider here, the question of *synchronic* unity, unity at the one time.

3.3.3.1. The synchronic unity of the bundle.   Suppose you have a number of 'perceptions', mental items, occurring at the same time: What makes them part of the same bundle? At a certain time, I have perception 1 and perception 2, while at the same time *you* have perception 3 and perception 4. What makes the first and second item 'go together', the third and fourth 'go together', but, at the same time, determines that the two little bundles are not parts of a single bigger bundle?

One thing that would solve this problem for Hume (and, indeed, solve the diachronic problem also) would be a suitably close causal relation to a particular human body: All your perceptions are causally linked to your body; all my perceptions are causally linked to my body. In a way, this solution pushes off the problem only to raise another one: What is the unity principle for sameness of my body and the sameness of your body? But this problem would seem to be at least easier to solve than the original 'bundle of perceptions' problem.

Interestingly, Hume does accept this solution for a much smaller and far less important problem: Why we speak of one and the same sound over time: "A man who hears a noise, that is frequently interrupted and renewed, says, it is still the same noise, though it is evident the sounds have only a specific identity or resemblance, and there is nothing numerically the same, but the cause, which produced them" (bk. 1, pt. IV, sec. VI). Here Hume is saying that the sound borrows its identity over time from the source of the sound, the cause that produced it. So why could he not say that the bundle of perceptions, the bundle of mental items, borrows its identity from the body that produces those particular perceptions?

Hume, however, never even considers trying to solve his problem about the bundle of perceptions in this way. I think that this is because Hume is such a thoroughgoing Dualist. The trouble with tying the bundle to a particular body is that this would make it impossible, self-contradictory, for the bundle to exist as a bundle in the absence of the body. If the bundle is a bundle because it is tied to a particular body, then the absence of a body entails that there is no bundle. I think it seemed obvious to Hume that a disembodied mind is a possibility. He was, it seems, an atheist and did not believe that the mind could in fact survive the dissolution of the physical body. But he did not think that there was any actual contradiction in the idea that the mind could survive the body. (And, indeed, I think Hume was right here.)

Combining the view that there is no contradiction in the notion that the mind can survive the body with the view that the mind is a bundle of non-physical perceptions creates a difficult problem for Hume. It means that he has got to find something *internal* to the bundle, some inner relation holding among the members of each bundle, that ties each bundle together. And that proves difficult.

If we concentrate first on the synchronic problem—unity at a particular time, the problem that Hume does not even seem to notice—it is difficult to see what solution Hume could have given except to say that there is a relation, call it *co-consciousness*, a relation that we are all acquainted with, but are unable to define further; a relation that holds between different mental items going on in the one mind at the one time. It isn't much of a solution, but it is hard to

see what else to do. You find this solution to the problem of synchronic unity appearing in the works of various philosophers after
Hume who were attracted to his bundle view.

3.3.3.2. The diachronic unity of the bundle.   Let us leave aside the
synchronic unity problem and turn to the even harder diachronic
problem. Some philosophers have thought that we might use
memory to unite the bundle of mental items over time. Let us
assume that the memory in question is event-memory, memory of
individual events, as opposed to remembering a bit of information,
say that Ulan Bator is the capital of Mongolia. And, to keep the
relation inside the bundle, let us assume that the events remembered
are our own earlier 'perceptions'. The idea that the only sort of
event we can remember directly (without any admixture of
inference) is some past mental state of our own is one that has at
least a bit of plausibility. But there is still the difficulty that we do
not remember a great deal of what went on in our minds in the past.
As Hume says: "It will be incumbent on those who affirm that
memory produces entirely our personal identity, to give a reason
why we can thus extend our identity beyond our memory" (bk. 1,
pt. IV, sec. VI).

The Scottish philosopher Thomas Reid reinforced Hume's point
here with the following case. The old general can remember himself
doing brave deeds as a young officer. The young officer could remember himself as a schoolboy being flogged for stealing apples.
But the general cannot remember the stealing of the apples. (See
Reid, *Inquiry and Essays*, pp. 217–218.)

Actually, Hume and Reid may be a bit too tough here. Something might be done with indirect memory links, which is what we
have in Reid's case. Start with the co-consciousness relation between items that occur at a certain time. To get everything in, let
this time be the instant that this mind ceases to exist. Now consider
the co-consciousness group that existed a short time before that. It
is plausible that the later, final group will contain a memory of
some item in the earlier group; and then that some item in the earlier group (not necessarily the same item) will contain a memory of
some item in a still earlier group; and so back and back to the first
moment of that mind's existence. You would then get what logi-
cians and mathematicians call a recursive relation, an indirect,

links-in-a-chain relation, that could stretch from the old general back to the schoolboy.

This idea is clever; but it still seems possible, empirically possible, to have co-consciousness groups that are, intuitively, part of a certain mind but that are not linked by memory in a suitable fashion. For instance, you half-wake up briefly in the night but have no memory of this event at all in the morning. The only way to link these experiences to the bundle as a whole would be for these nighttime mental happenings to contain a memory of past experience. They may perhaps contain such a memory. But do they *have* to do so in order to make the nighttime items part of your mind? It does not seem so.

Hume tries to solve his problem differently. He appeals to three different principles that, he thinks, influence our imagination in treating things that exist at different times as stages of just one thing. These principles are:

1. resemblance
2. contiguity in space and time
3. causation

Hume then points out that (2) is not relevant here. The 'perceptions' are, according to him, not in physical space; so there cannot be contiguity in space; and because of sound sleep and such, the bundle has only an intermittent existence, thus cutting out contiguity in time. So Hume is restricted to resemblance and causation.

It is clear that there will be certain resemblances between earlier and later stages of the one bundle. From day to day our perceptions, emotions, and thoughts will normally be rather similar. But only normally. Sometimes we have quite novel sensations, emotions, and thoughts. Yet we recognize easily that these 'perceptions' are part of our mind. Lack of resemblance is no bar. So it seems that Hume must put the greatest weight on *causation*, rather than resemblance, and that is just what he does:

> Our impressions give rise to their correspondent ideas; and these ideas in their turn, produce other impressions, one thought chases another, and draws after it a third, by which it is expelled in its turn.

> In this respect, I cannot compare the soul more properly to anything than to a republic or commonwealth, in which the several members are united by the reciprocal ties of government and subordination, and give rise to other persons who propagate the same republic in the incessant changes of its parts. And as the same individual republic may not only change its members, but also its laws and constitutions; in like manner the same person may vary his character and disposition, as well as his impressions and ideas, without losing his identity. Whatever changes he endures, his several parts are still connected by the relation of causation. (bk. 1, pt. IV, sec. VI)

In the Appendix to the *Treatise*, however, Hume tells us that this solution will not work, but he does not tell us why it fails. The general thought must be that it is possible that certain mental items are part of the mind but are not causally related in the desired way. Here is an imaginary case that perhaps is an instance of this possibility. Suppose that a certain person has the following power: Just by mental concentration, the individual can cause another person to feel a pain. The idea is that there should be 'direct', unmediated, causal connection between A's mental act and B's pain. It is clear from the description of the case that the pain is in B's mind. It is B that has the pain. But if causal connection is the main principle of unity of the mind—is of the essence of a bundle-mind—then would we not have to say that the pain was in A's mind?

It seems likely, therefore, that if the mind is reduced to a bundle of immaterial 'perceptions', then it will not be possible to discover a satisfactory bundling formula. And in any case, as we have also seen, the items in the bundle do not appear to be 'distinct existences', substances in their own right; rather they appear to be entities that demand a substance of which they can be dependents, for instance as attributes. Such a substance would also provide a solution to the bundling problem, thus killing two birds. And I think, for all Hume shows, that it could be a material substance.

Readings and references for Hume

Chappell, V. C., ed. 1996. *Hume: A Collection of Critical Essays*. New York: Anchor. See in particular, T. Penelhum, "Hume on Personal Identity".

Garett, D. 1981. "Hume's Self-Doubts About Personal Identity", *Philosophical Review* 90: pp.337–358.

Hume, David. 1739. *A Treatise of Human Nature*. Reprint, ed. Ernest C. Mossner. Great Britain: Penguin Books, 1969.

Laird, John. 1932. *Hume's Philosophy of Human Nature*. London: Methuen. See chapter 5, "Bodies and Minds".

McNabb, D.G.C. 1951. *David Hume*. London: Hutchinson. See chapter 9. This book is especially recommended for its clarity.

Norton, David Fate, Nicholas Capaldi, and Wade L. Robison, eds. 1979. *McGill Hume Studies*. San Diego: Austin Hill Press. See the papers by McIntyre, Robison, and Wilson.

Reid, Thomas. 1975. *Inquiry and Essays*, ed. Keith Lehrer and Ronald E. Beanblossom. Indianapolis: The Library of Living Arts.

Twentieth century discussion of the Bundle theory

For

Ayer, A. J. 1956. *The Problem of Knowledge*. London: Macmillan. See chapter 5.

Against

Armstrong, D. M. 1993. *A Materialist Theory of the Mind*. London: Routledge. See chapter 2, sections II and III.

CHAPTER FOUR

T. H. Huxley's Epiphenomenalism

The text for this section is Thomas Huxley's article "On the Hypothesis That Animals Are Automata, and Its History". Huxley's paper is written with great clarity and is the best possible introduction to Epiphenomenalism as it emerged in the nineteenth century. It is, however, not easily available. So it is reprinted, somewhat abridged, as an appendix to this volume.

The first section of this chapter is a running analysis of Huxley's argument. That argument first goes back to Descartes' doctrine of the brute-machine, the idea that nonhuman animals are nothing more than mechanical automata, lacking any consciousness. Huxley argues that the evidence for this view is quite strong, but in the end he rejects it because he cannot believe that the animals are so utterly unlike us, who *are* conscious. Nevertheless, he thinks that there was something right about Descartes' position. The consciousness that we have, and that the other animals have to a degree, is completely *powerless*. As a result, it is unable to act upon the body in any way. After outlining Huxley's argument, we will proceed to criticize it. Mention will be made of contemporary philosophers who have views similar to Huxley's.

4.1. Huxley's argument

4.1.1. (pp. 145 to 146) The body is a purely physical mechanism
Huxley begins with the physicalizing of biology. He says:

In the seventeenth century, the idea that the physical processes of life are capable of being explained in the same way as other physical phenomena, and, therefore, that the living body is a mechanism, was proved to be true for certain classes of vital actions; and, having thus taken firm root in irrefragable fact, this conception has not only successfully repelled every assault that has been made upon it, but has steadily grown in force and application, until it is now the expressed or implied fundamental proposition of the whole doctrine of scientific Physiology.

Huxley says that there were two great pioneers. First, William Harvey (who established the circulation of the blood, pumped by the heart) began to show us how the body sustains itself and reproduces. Second, somewhat less appreciated, there was Descartes with his work on sensation and motion.

4.1.2. (pp. 147 to 150) A change in the brain state is the invariable antecedent of all mental occurrence

Descartes argued, and, says Huxley, it is now established, that the brain is the 'seat' of all forms of consciousness. It is important to realize that, despite his somewhat misleading use of the word 'seat', Huxley is definitely not arguing that consciousness is a process in the brain. Huxley remains a Dualist. His idea is that the brain is the immediate cause of mental phenomena. But he holds that the mental phenomena themselves, the effects of purely physical happenings in the brain, are not physical. Notice also the identification of the mental with consciousness. Like Hume, who influenced him, Huxley is still working in the Cartesian tradition, although he is trying to work away from it.

4.1.3. (p. 150) Soul or bundle of phenomena?

Huxley then offers us a choice between Descartes and Hume, between spiritual substance and a bundle of perceptions:

For of two alternatives one must be true. Either consciousness is the function of something distinct from the brain, which we call the soul, and a sensation is the mode in which this soul is affected by the motion of a part of the brain; or there is no soul, and a sensation is something generated by the mode of motion of a part of the brain. In the former case, the phenomena of the senses are purely spiritual affections; in the latter, they are something manufactured by the mechanism of the body and as unlike the causes which set that mechanism in motion, as the sound of a repeater [a watch or clock that strikes] is unlike the pushing of the spring which gives rise to it.

Although Huxley does not say so at this point, his own view is the second one, Hume's view.

4.1.4. (p.150 to p.151) Reflex action

Huxley then draws attention to the notion of a reflex action, a notion that, he points out, was quite well understood by Descartes. It is bodily action that appears to bypass the mind. He quotes from Descartes:

If someone moves his hand rapidly toward our eyes, as if he were going to strike us, although we know he is a friend, that he does it only in jest, and that he will be very careful to do us no harm, nevertheless it will be hard to keep from winking. And this shows, that it is not by the agency of the soul that the eyes shut, since the action is contrary to that volition which is the only, or at least the chief function of the soul; but it is because the mechanism of our body is so disposed, that the motion of the hand towards the eyes excites another movement in our brain, and this sends the animal spirits into those muscles which cause the eyelids to close.

This, says Huxley, is the same general conception of reflex action that we still have.

4.1.5. (p.151 to p.152) The dependence of memory on traces left in the brain

This doctrine is to be found in Descartes. Huxley says that it is fully established, although, of course, the Cartesian details have to be changed. But it is really the beginning of a big retreat from Dualism when memory, which is surely a psychological matter, is referred to the brain for its cause.

4.1.6. (p.153 to p.161) The Cartesian doctrine of the brute-machine

This highly controversial Cartesian doctrine states that the brutes (the nonhuman animals) lack not only reason but also consciousness. Given Descartes' view that consciousness is the essence of mentality, this doctrine entails that these animals lack mentality altogether. When we fall forward, Descartes points out, we automatically throw our hands forward to save our face (cf. the winking reflex, already mentioned). Descartes then argues: "All the actions of beasts are similar only to those which we perform without the help of our minds." When light is reflected from the body of a wolf into the eye of a sheep, the sheep flees. It is natural to say that it fears the wolf, and it flees because it fears. But fearing is something mental, and for Descartes nothing mental at all goes on in the sheep. It is not conscious, and therefore it has no mind. The light from the body of the wolf stirs the sheep to reflex action only. That is all the sheep (or the wolf for that matter) is capable of doing.

Why did Descartes embrace this strange position? It was because consciousness—mind, for him—was a property, *the* property, of souls. And he had good theological reasons for denying that beasts had any souls. But philosophically he looks to be on shaky ground here, as generations of later philosophers have not failed to point out. (See 4.1.7. below.)

Huxley, however, proceeds to argue that the evidence for the brute-machine view is actually much stronger than it was in Descartes' day. This sounds paradoxical until we see, as we will shortly, how Huxley's argument will go. The evidence he alludes to falls into three parts: cases in the brain where the connection between the brain and the spinal cord has been severed; cases in frogs where a large portion of the brain has been removed; finally, the strange case of Sergeant F_.

4.1.6.1. The spinal cord cases. In cases where the connection of spinal cord to brain has been severed, the cord still has remarkable reflex powers. Tickling the soles of the feet, for instance, causes the legs to be drawn up:

> In order to move the legs in this way, a definite co-ordination of muscular contractions is necessary; the muscles must contract in a certain order and with duly proportionate force; and moreover, as [since] the

feet are drawn away from the source of the irritation, it may be said that the action has a final cause, or is purposive.

4.1.6.2. The frog. Similar reflex powers are exhibited by a frog with a severed spinal cord, a severing that cuts off the frog's legs from its brain. If an irritant is applied to the side of its body, the frog's legs will be impelled to rub at the irritated point. Again, a frog whose front brain has been removed, so that it surely cannot have any consciousness, will not in general react to stimuli. But if thrown into water it goes through all the complex motions of swimming, just as well as a frog whose brain is intact.

4.1.6.3. Sergeant F_. But Huxley's exhibit A, as it were, in support of the brute-machine hypothesis is the French sergeant wounded in the head during the Franco–Prussian war in 1870. This man, whose case is described at length by Huxley, passed from time to time into a state of automatism, where he seemed like a sleep walker. But during these episodes he remained capable of a good many of the actions of ordinary life.

I don't think this case supports Huxley's argument in the way he thinks it does; so I will not give much time to it. Sergeant F_ shows abundant signs of mental life in his strange states; for instance he can eat, dress, and sing songs that he knows. His actions seem not to be just reflex actions, as Huxley wants to argue. It is true that, on the evidence given, he seems not to be *conscious* during these episodes. But this fact, I suggest, should lead us to question Huxley's Cartesian assumption that consciousness is the essence of mentality. You can have mental processes without consciousness; and it is likely that is what was happening in the case of the sergeant.

4.1.7. (p.161 to p.162) Huxley's rejection of the brute-machine

Although Huxley thinks that the evidence for Descartes' strange doctrine is even stronger than the evidence available in Descartes' day, he nevertheless rejects the idea of the brute-machine. He argues that it is too implausible that humans, alone among the animals, should have consciousness: "The doctrine of continuity is too well established for it to be permissible for me to suppose that any natural phenomenon comes into existence suddenly, and without being preceded by simpler modifications."

This argument, based on the way animals have evolved over millions of years, is undoubtedly a good one. But Huxley seems unaware that it also poses a long-term threat to his own position. Materialists can without difficulty allow continuity between living beings that have no mental life—plants, single cell creatures—and those with a primitive mental life—perhaps the insects, who at least seem to have perceptions and purposes—and finally with those having a mental life that involves consciousness—perhaps the mammals, or at any rate the higher mammals. For the Materialist, this continuity is just a matter of increasingly greater complexity and sophistication of the physical processes involved. But a Dualist, even a Bundle Dualist, has to postulate a point, both in evolutionary development and in the development of the individual, where non-physical mental phenomena first appear. Whatever point is postulated, it will seem rather arbitrary. And how are you going to get continuity between the physical and the non-physical?

It should be noted, though, that some Dualist thinkers have tried to meet the 'continuity problem' by denying that there really is any break of continuity. As you go back to less and less complex organisms, they suggest, you *do* find non-physical mentality. It is just that it is of a more and more unsophisticated sort, which does not easily reveal itself. Indeed, some have suggested that all matter has a non-physical mental side. This theory is called Panpsychism (mind everywhere). These hypotheses answer the continuity objection, but at the cost of postulating schemes for which there seems to be little *independent* evidence.

4.1.8. (p.162 to p.163) Animals have consciousness, but are automata

It is clear, says Huxley, that motions in the brain precede consciousness, and he says that this fact may be taken as good evidence that the motions cause consciousness. (Huxley, like Hume, is not worried about matter in motion causing something that is non-physical.) But, he asks: "Is there any evidence that these states of consciousness may, conversely cause those molecular changes which give rise to molecular motion. *I see no such evidence*" (my italics).

The brain, Huxley thinks, is perfectly competent to bring about all the behaviour of an animal. (What an advance towards Materialism here!) He says: "The consciousness of brutes . . . [is] as completely without any power of modifying that working [their behaviour] as the steam-whistle which accompanies the work of a locomotive engine is without influence on its machinery." For 'brutes', then, Huxley has reached what philosophers call Epiphenomenalism. Their mental lives are bundles of impotent perceptions. Hume's bundles could act on the body, presumably through the brain. Huxley's bundles cannot.

4.1.9. (p.163 to end) And the same applies to man

It remains only for Huxley to extend this doctrine to mankind. Even in human beings, there is no reason to think that the 'bundle of perceptions' has any physical effect. For instance: "The feeling we call volition is not the cause of a voluntary act, but the symbol of that state of the brain which is the immediate cause of the act." Huxley quotes at length another Epiphenomenalist, Charles Bonnet, who says that "the soul is a mere spectator of the movements of its body", although "it believes itself to be the author of them". The Appendix to this book ends with the passage from Bonnet.

4.2. Critique of Epiphenomenalism

4.2.1. Why did consciousness evolve?

An objection often made against Epiphenomenalism is based on the theory of evolution by natural selection. What is selected is, in general, whatever aids survival, because survivors can have descendants. But if consciousness is impotent, why should it ever have evolved? It cannot aid survival.

The objection can be answered. The Epiphenomenalist can suggest that consciousness is a *causal by-product* of evolution. The complex organization of the brain that the higher animals possess was selected because it *did* confer evolutionary advantage: the advantage of being the cause of more sophisticated behaviour. But, the Epiphenomenalist can argue, it so happens that this sort of superior organization in the brain inevitably, by the laws of nature, brings with it as a side-product the evolutionarily useless consciousness.

Frank Jackson, in his paper "Epiphenomenal Qualia", has given the example of the polar bear's coat. For a bear that lived in particularly cold regions, this thick coat gave the advantage of warmth, and so it was selected. But the thickness needed for the warmth inevitably brings with it extra weight to carry around, which is no advantage at all; indeed it is presumably some slight disadvantage. Consciousness, on Huxley's theory, is like the weight of the coat, indeed it is a little better than that because, although it gives no evolutionary advantage, it also gives no evolutionary disadvantage.

4.2.2. Strange laws

But this reply, although it does meet the evolutionary objection, does so by making it clear how peculiar are the laws of nature that the Epiphenomenalist has to countenance. There is no *contradiction* in there being laws of the sort that he or she has to postulate, but they are strange. There are two strange features about them.

The first odd feature is shared with Dualisms that are not Epiphenomenal, that is, are Interactionist. For the rest of nature, it seems plausible to say, the laws of physics are the only fundamental laws that we need to postulate. But in one small corner of the universe, or perhaps in a few such small corners if there is mentality elsewhere, new fundamental laws have to be introduced. These laws link certain physical conditions that hold in the central nervous systems of certain organisms with certain mental entities: sensations, thoughts, purposes, and so on. Given certain physical conditions, certain mental states are caused to come into existence. The new laws must be fundamental, or at least must be consequences of new fundamental laws, because there is nothing in the rest of natural science from which these psycho-physical laws can be deduced or in any way explained. The new laws have to be tacked on to the structure of the physical laws in a quite arbitrary way.

But the laws are even stranger than this. The physical conditions that give rise to, say, a pain are incredibly complex interrelations of huge numbers of neurons, and the neurons themselves are exceedingly complex physical entities. The pain itself, Dualists will presumably want to say, is a relatively simple entity. That is what introspection seems to show us. A hugely complex physical entity gives rise to a rather simple mental entity, and this relationship is supposed to be, or to reflect, an extra and fundamental law. Do we want to postulate such laws? (The important points made here were made by J.J.C. Smart in his famous article "Sensations and Brain Processes", which we will meet again in the chapter on the Identity theory.)

To these law-related implausibilities Epiphenomenalism adds a second and still stranger feature. The mental entities have a feature that is not met with anywhere else in the natural world: They have absolutely no causal effects whatsoever. They are totally impotent. This claim seems wrong. If the physical brings the mental into existence, then everything we know of the way of the world tells us that the mental will itself have effects. Indeed, the mental ought to react back on its cause; for Newton's third law, the law that action and reaction are equal and opposite, is thought to hold throughout the natural world. Yet here there is said to be action in nature without any reaction at all. We ought to be suspicious of this claim.

4.2.3. We experience the action of mind on body

Are we not directly aware of the action of the mind on the body? We feel pain or we think certain thoughts. Are we not aware that, as a causal consequence, the body tenses up, or certain sounds issue from our mouths?

I think that, indeed, we are aware of this relationship between mind and body. Unfortunately, however, Epiphenomenalists can explain the situation away as an illusion, and they can give a fairly plausible explanation of the illusion. The source of the illusion, they will say, is this: There is a regular experience of, say, pain, followed by an experience of tensing. But in the state of nature, before we arrive at Epiphenomenalism, we are unaware that the real cause of the tensing is not the pain but a process in the brain. Indeed, in the state of nature, it will be rational to explain the regular sequence of pain followed by physical tensing as a causal sequence. In fact, though, the Epiphenomenalist says, the brain process causes both the pain and the bodily tensing. But because the pain precedes the bodily tensing, the pain seems to us to be the cause of the tensing. The illusion persists even when we know better, that is, when we become Epiphenomenalists.

This seems a satisfactory answer. There might be some difficulty for one who wanted to combine Epiphenomenalism with a regular succession view of causality; for, by hypothesis, we do have a regular succession: pain → physical tensing.

4.2.4. Can the Epiphenomenalist account for our knowledge of other minds?

What good reasons do we have to think that others besides ourselves have consciousness? One way that we can argue is like this: I am aware of being in pain. I seem to be aware that the pain has made me groan. So when another groans, I can account for this groan by the explanatory hypothesis that it is caused in the same sort of way that my groan is: by a pain. But if I decide that my pain does not cause my groan, that is, if I decide that Huxley's theory is true, this inference becomes lost to me. All I seem to be able to infer is that something in the other person's brain causes the groan. Why should I infer that the other has a conscious experience like mine? In the same way, I lose the inference from the speech-like sounds that others utter to what is on their mind.

The following argument may perhaps do better. It is a form of the traditional argument for other minds, known as the Argument from Analogy. The argument starts from the likeness that we find between other human bodies and ourselves, in particular the deep likenesses in behaviour. This is the analogy, and it is there despite all sorts of differences between one human being and another. Now we find in our own case that there are all sorts of apparently law-like connections between our behaviour and our mental states. We get cut or hit, and we feel pain. We feel pain, and we carry on in various familiar ways. We see others cut or hit, and then we see them carry on in the same familiar ways. Is it not a good hypothesis that these others have pain like ourselves?

This is quite a good rational argument for the existence of other minds, although I think it is not quite as convincing as the causal argument considered a paragraph before. But *for the Epiphenomenalist* a difficulty remains. Suppose for instance that somebody tells me that they have a toothache. If I accept Epiphenomenalism, am I not forced to reason that it is the person's brain processes that are causing those noises to come out of their mouth? Hence cannot I reason that *even if the speaker did not have any pain*, that person would still have uttered the same words? But if that is so, have I any reason to believe that the person really is in pain?

The Epiphenomenalist is not without resources here, but the argument gets difficult. It may be better to pass on to a still more radical difficulty.

4.2.5. Can Epiphenomenalists know they themselves have mental states?

What of my knowledge that I myself have mental states? Can I justify this knowledge if I am an Epiphenomenalist? I must accept that my belief that I have mental states is caused by a brain state and not by any mental state. Consider first my belief that in the past I had mental states. Have I any reason to accept this belief? After all, I would have had this belief even if I had had no such states but still had the current brain state that is causing my belief. So what justification have I for believing in these past mental states? It is not at all clear. Perhaps it is just a deception foisted upon me by my brain.

Am I even justified in believing that I am currently having any mental states? Presumably, this line of argument cannot be used against the belief itself. But for my other current mental states, may not my brain-caused belief be a false one? I would still have it even if that belief was my only actual current mental state.

The second part of this argument would no doubt have been rejected by Huxley, who would have followed Hume in holding that we cannot be mistaken about the exact current contents of the bundle. But if a mistake is possible even about current contents, as most philosophers now concede, then perhaps Epiphenomenalism should make one sceptical of the existence of the greatest part of one's own contents of consciousness. Epiphenomenalism seems to push us towards Eliminativism, the view that minds are just a myth. (We will examine the Eliminativist view in Chapter 8.)

4.3. Summing up on Epiphenomenalism

Perhaps enough reasons have now been given to show that Epiphenomenalism is a rather implausible position. Huxley is really a thinker in an intellectual *bind*. His science drives him toward a physicalistic account of human beings. At the same time, the philosophy of his day, almost to a thinker, held to a Dualist philosophy of mind and so denied that the mind is something physical. Huxley himself was profoundly influenced by Descartes and Hume. His Epiphenomenalism was what we might think of as a somewhat desperate attempt to reconcile Materialism with Dualism. Let the brain do all the work. Let it be the cause of everything the body does and everything the mind does. So much he concedes to Materialism, and it is indeed a great deal to concede. But he throws the Dualists quite a big bone also. The mental itself, though having its sole cause in the brain, is not something material. But to make the compromise work he has to deny that the mental has any effect on the brain. It has all the look of an *unstable* compromise.

Huxley is not the last of the Epiphenomenalists, though in our day Epiphenomenalists tend to turn over more and more of the mental to the material side, to the brain. In our day Frank Jackson and Keith Campbell argued at one time that the *sensible qualities* we meet with in perception, sensation, and imagery, though produced by the brain, have no causal power to act. (Colour is the traditional example.) But that is as far as their Epiphenomenalism went. Beliefs and purposes they took to be physical states and processes in the brain. But the position they retreated to—a minimal Epiphenomenalism, we might call it—still has quite serious difficulties. It is interesting to notice that both thinkers have since abandoned even this minimal position.

For both Jackson and Campbell *beliefs* were assumed to be purely physical states of the brain. So what about the belief that there are such things as the experiencing of sensible qualities? They both believed this to be true. (As most of us do!) But they also accepted that the physical states of the brain that produced that belief in the experience (itself a physical state of the brain) would have produced that belief *even if there were no sensible qualities to experience.* So did they have any good reason to believe in these qualities?

Readings and references for Huxley

Campbell, Keith. 1984. *Body and Mind.* 2d Rev. ed. Indiana: University of Notre Dame Press. See chapter 7, "A New Epiphenomenalism".

Chalmers, David. 1996. *The Conscious Mind.* New York and Oxford: Oxford University Press. This anti-Materialist work is one of the most interesting books on the philosophy of mind published in recent years. Chalmers is not an Epiphenomenalist, but his position steers close to it, and in any case he holds that it does not have any fatal flaws. Sections 4.2.4 and 4.2.5 above raise questions that are discussed in depth by Chalmers. See, in particular, part 2 of his book.

James, William. 1950. *The Principles of Psychology.* USA: Dover Publications. See volume 1, chapter 5, "The Automaton-Theory".

Jackson, Frank. 1982. "Epiphenomenal Qualia." *Philosophical Quarterly* 30: pp. 147–155. Reprinted in William G. Lycan, *Mind and Cognition.* Cambridge, Mass:. Blackwell, 1990. Section IV, titled "The Bogey of

Epiphenomenalism," of Jackson's article is the important one for the discussion of this chapter.

Criticism of Jackson

Churchland, P. M. 1985. "Reduction, Qualia, and the Direct Inspection of Brain States." *Journal of Philosophy* 82 (1985): pp. 8–28.

Horgan, T. 1984. "Jackson on Physical Information and Qualia." *Philosophical Quarterly* 34: pp. 147–155.

Lewis, David. 1990. "What Experience Teaches." In Lycan, *Mind and Cognition*, pp. 499–518.

Lycan, William G. 1990. *Mind and Cognition*. Cambridge, Mass:. Blackwell. Further responses to Jackson may be found in section 17.

A reply by Jackson

Jackson, Frank. 1986. "What Mary Didn't Know." *Journal of Philosophy* 83: pp. 291–295.

Smart, J.J.C. 1959. "Sensations and Brain Processes." *Philosophical Review* 68: pp.141–156. Reprinted often.

CHAPTER FIVE

Ryle's Rejection of Two Realms

The text for this chapter is Gilbert Ryle's The Concept of Mind, *any edition. His first chapter lays out the main theme. See also Jaegwon Kim,* Philosophy of Mind, *chapter 2, "Mind As Behavior: Behaviorism".*

Ryle's book was published in 1949 and for the next twenty years or so was the most influential contemporary work on the philosophy of mind. His official opponent is Descartes, and Ryle has a tendency to treat philosophy of mind as a matter of Descartes versus Ryle! Section 1 of chapter 1, "The Official Doctrine", gives a lively, if hostile, account of the Cartesian view. Ryle calls that view, with 'deliberate abusiveness', he says, 'the dogma of the Ghost in the Machine'. The phrase has stuck.

But Ryle is really taking on something much more general than Cartesian Dualism. He is rejecting the view that the mind and body are two entities on the same level, like a knife and a fork, or, more to the point, like car engine and car body, with the mind as a sort of engine to the body. This has been the theme of the views that we have looked at so far: The mind is a thing alongside the body. Descartes, Hume, and Huxley all think of the mind as immaterial, not in physical space. But for Ryle the alleged immateriality of the mind is not the central point. From time to time in the discussion so far we have contrasted these Immaterialist views with the Materialist view that the mind is to be identified with a particular part of the body: the brain. This view is equally unacceptable to Ryle. As Ryle sees it, this view substitutes the Machine in the Machine for the Ghost in the Machine. Ryle seems to think that the Machine is just as bad as the Ghost.

Hume broke the Ghost up into a bundle of immaterial 'perceptions'. But the bundle can still be thought of as a thing. The assemblage of perceptions still exists alongside the body and animates the body. Huxley, it must be admitted, does do something more radical. He cuts the causal link from the bundle to the body. This is a move away from the general position that Ryle is attacking: the mind as inner cause of mind-betokening activities. But Huxley does this only because of empirical difficulties. He does not, as Ryle does, think that it is an incoherent or senseless notion that the mental should act on the physical. Huxley is happy to admit that the mental *seems* to act on the body. He holds merely that the mind does not act physically as a matter of empirical fact.

5.1. Mind–body interaction a category-mistake

As Ryle emphasizes in section 2 of chapter 1, he thinks that the whole idea of mind–body interaction is a *category-mistake*. He gives some examples of such mistakes: (1) A visitor to Oxford sees the colleges, the libraries, the playing fields, the museums, the scientific departments, the administrative offices. But afterwards he says "But where is the university?" (It is helpful to know that Oxford University is spread out round the town.) (2) A child sees the battalions, batteries, squadrons, and so on of an army division march past. Afterwards he wants to know when the division will march past. (3) A Frenchman is taken to a game of cricket, and the function of various players is pointed out to him. He is told what bowlers, batsmen, wicket-keepers and so on are supposed to do. Afterwards he asks "But whose function is it to exercise the famous team spirit?" Such persons, says Ryle, have not made empirical but *conceptual* mistakes: "Their puzzles arise from an inability to use certain items in the English vocabulary."

Ryle thinks that we know well enough how to employ mental concepts in everyday speech. But when we theorize about the mind, at any rate since Descartes, we fall into category error, in particular the error of the two-realm story. We are like people who understand talk about 'the average taxpayer' well enough in practical talk, but who, when asked who the average taxpayer really is, still think of that person as a certain individual who we might, for instance, meet at a party. (Notice, as Kim Sterelny has pointed out, that this commits Ryle to thinking that there is quite a sharp division between employing mental concepts in our practical talk and theorizing about them. Of course there is such a division, but perhaps it is not as sharp as Ryle thinks.)

What is Ryle's own story about mind and body? The cases of the university and the army division suggest that Ryle thinks that a two-realm story falls into error by taking the same thing twice over (metaphysical double-vision, as we might say); that in turn suggests that for Ryle mental activity is nothing but a certain subclass of bodily activities. Ryle, it seems, leans towards Behaviourism, where the mind cannot be the *cause* of behaviour because it *is* behaviour. From the 1920s to the 1960s Behaviourism was an important influence in psychology and philosophy. And there certainly seems to be a push towards Behaviourism in Ryle's book. But, confusingly, Ryle denies that he is a Behaviourist. This denial, however, may have two causes: (1) Ryle's avowed hostility to all 'isms'; and (2) his magnification of minor differences with Behaviourism in the interest of product differentiation.

The cricket case is harder to interpret. Ryle says team spirit is the keenness with which individual cricketing tasks are performed; it is not itself a further task. What point does he want to make about the mental concepts? I think that he may be pointing to a special *dispositional* element that is present when mental concepts are used to describe behaviour. More about dispositions later.

5.2. Is the will a cause?

It is, as already noted, an essential part of Ryle's view to reject what he calls the para-mechanical myth (if he were directing his main fire against the Materialists it would be the mechanical myth), namely, that mental events, states, and processes are causes of bodily events, states, and processes. That is the two-realm, the two-thing, picture, a picture that he thinks is quite wrong.

We will take as our illustrative example Ryle's rejection of a Causal theory of the will. Ryle rejects this theory in chapter 3, where he tries to destroy it by using an infinite regress argument.

It will help to focus things if we start from a point made by Ludwig Wittgenstein (*Philosophical Investigations*, sec. 62). We can distinguish between bodily actions, things that a person does (and so may be morally responsible for), and mere bodily happenings. Consider:

1. He raised his arm.
2. His arm rose.

Wittgenstein points out that the truth of (1) actually entails the truth of (2), but that the truth of (2) fails to entail the truth of (1). Consider, for instance, the case where his arm rose, not because he meant to raise it, but because it got entangled with a rope going up. Wittgenstein further notes that this enables the problem of the nature of action to be formulated in a particularly sharp way. What condition must be added to mere bodily happening (the arm going up) to yield bodily action (his raising his arm)? What condition must be added to (2) to give (1)? (Compare Plato's classical formulation of the problem of the definition of knowledge. Knowledge entails true belief, but true belief does not entail knowledge. What condition, then, must be added to true belief to give knowledge?)

There is a traditional answer to the problem of saying what a true action is. According to this view it is an action, as opposed to a mere bodily happening, if and only if it is caused by a certain sort of mental cause, often called a volition or an act of willing. This view presupposes that there are such inner mental causes. Ryle, of course, wants to deny this. He advances a number of arguments against the traditional theory, but the one that rightly secured the most attention is his ingenious attempt to construct a *destructive dilemma* for this answer.

Consider again raising the arm. This is supposed to be a matter of willing the arm to go up, a willing that causes the arm to go up. But, Ryle says, either this willing is an action (a mental action) of the person, or it is not. Taking either horn of this dilemma leads to trouble. Suppose, first, willing is a (mental) action. Then, by the very theory under consideration, this action will have to be caused by a further willing, which will demand a still further willing, and so on, ad infinitum. This situation is impossible. (Ryle uses a lot of these *infinite regress* arguments in his book.) But suppose instead that the first willing is *not* an action. Then, argues Ryle, since the willing is not willed, it is just something that happens in the mind that causes the arm to move. And how then can you say that what it brings about is a real *action*? Since the willing just happens, since it just pops up in the mind without the person having any control over it, the person can't help the willing, and so can't help the arm going up. Hence the arm going up is not really an action. Whichever horn you take, the Causal theory is reduced to absurdity.

The infinite regress involved in the first horn of the dilemma looks conclusive. For a long time I thought it was conclusive. Actually, a subtle answer to it has been given by Daniel Dennett, but I won't discuss that answer until much later in the book (see section 9.2.1 in the chapter on Functionalism). I will content myself here with trying to show that the second horn is not so sharp as it looks. (I don't think it ever looked as sharp as the first one.)

The vital point is that willing is a quite special sort of mental cause. To be a willing it must spring from *further mental causes*, in particular from our desires, from our perceptions, from our knowledge, practical and theoretical, and from our beliefs. It must spring from, be caused by, things that we want, things that we currently perceive (or misperceive) about our current situation, things that we know or believe about that situation, and things that we know and believe about ways to get what we want. We act by willing to do something in the light of, as a result of, our desires, perceptions, and beliefs. That is the sort of mental cause that willing is.

Once we see this, then it becomes clear that there is no infinite regress of actions. For desires, perceptions, and beliefs are *not* actions. They are not things that we *do*, but things that we *have*. They have their causes, of course, but these causes will only sometimes include our own actions.

There remains a subsidiary difficulty. Talking about volitions and even about willing sounds pretty unnatural for most actions. I raise my arm, but just to get down a cup from the shelf. Did I will to raise my arm, or did I have a volition that raised my arm? It sounds a bit ridiculous. Ryle uses the unnaturalness of these idioms in criticising, and also making fun of, the Causal theory of action.

I think the Causal theory can do a bit better than this by substituting much more ordinary words. I suggest that if A does action P, then its cause is always A's *trying* or *attempting* to do P. (For more development, see Armstrong, 1981.) This way of putting it also sounds a bit strange at first hearing because most ordinary actions, such as getting the cup down, are casually and easily done without any trying or attempting in the sense of setting oneself deliberately to do the thing that was done.

Consider, however, what one would say if, during the reaching for the cup, one was unexpectedly struck by a sudden paralysis of the arm. One would surely describe this by saying that one had been trying to get the cup down. This fact strongly suggests that trying is always present in every action, however simple. It is normally *misleading* to speak of trying to do something routine because that suggests that the action is difficult to do, or that it is not certain that one will be able to do it, or perhaps even that failure is likely. But what is misleading to say can nevertheless be true to say. (This is quite an important point in semantics, in particular in the so-called *pragmatics* of speech.) It would be strange, and perhaps misleading, to say that every human being is over two inches in height. But it is nevertheless true. It is misleading to say that we believe we have heads on our shoulders, because that suggests that we don't know that we have them there. But it is true that we believe it, because we know it, and knowledge entails belief. So I think we can defend the view that any action of ours, to be an action, must have trying (attempting) to do that act as its cause. We don't need to talk about willing and still less do we need the term 'volition' if we do not like it.

5.3. The Argument from Distinct Existences

There is another important argument against the classical, causal account of action that is not used by Ryle but is deployed by some of those philosophers who were sympathetic to the Rylean approach (e.g., A. I. Melden in his book *Free Action*). Brian Medlin, in his paper "Ryle and the Mechanical Hypothesis", christened it 'The Argument from Distinct Existences'. Medlin's paper, incidentally, is the best criticism of Ryle's theory from a Materialist point of view that has been written.

The argument is that the supposed cause can be characterized only in terms of its effects. You go to raise your arm. On the Causal theory, a mental cause is operating. What is its nature? It is the arm-raising cause. If you had gone to move your leg instead, it would have been the leg-moving cause. The cause seems to be constituted by what it brings about. It is nothing in itself. A real cause, however, must be something in itself, distinct from its effect.[1]

This is an interesting argument, but it seems to confuse what we know of the cause with what the cause *is*. It confuses epistemology with ontology. The cause cannot be just that which brings about its effect. The cause must have a nature of its own independent of its effect. That is good ontology. But does this claim concerning the independent nature of a cause mean that we must be *aware* of that nature? We can hypothesize a cause that brings about an effect and call it the arm-raising cause for the time being. Later we may discover, or guess, its nature, for instance that it is spiritual or that it is physiological (or even sometimes the one, sometimes the other).

But what about the first-person case? When you raise your arm, you are, in normal cases at least, aware that you are raising it (it is not just going up). If asked about it, you will probably be able to say "Yes, I lifted my arm. I did not find it just going up." But if the Causal theory of action is true, you are aware of a mental cause of a special sort that has caused the arm to go up, but you are not aware of its concrete nature. Is this not paradoxical?

I don't think that it is all that paradoxical. Why should we not be introspectively aware of mental causes operating within us, be aware of the way in which they tend, but be unaware of their nature? A parallel case is our awareness of pressure on our body. Such pressure is causal action, tending to bring about a certain effect, the relative displacement of some part of our flesh. We are often aware, directly aware, of pressure on our body, but are not necessarily aware of the nature of the operating cause. Why should not our awareness of the operation of our own will be like this?

5.4. The importance of behaviour
for our concept of the mental

Although the 'Argument from Distinct Existences' seems not to be sound, it does bring out something extremely important about our mental concepts. Even if it is wrong to identify the mental with behaviour, still it appears that many, and perhaps all, of our mental concepts can be defined only by bringing behaviour in as part of their definition.

The role of behaviour is particularly conspicuous in the case of the will. We cannot understand what a trying is except in terms of what we are trying *to do*. Purposes can be explicated only in terms of the thing purposed, intentions in terms of the thing intended. You cannot say what your purpose *is* when you get a beer from the fridge without linking it to the behaviour (which may or may not actually occur) of going to the fridge and getting a suitable bottle out. Does this fact hold for all of the mental concepts? Do they all involve essential reference to behaviour? If so, this would explain the appeal of Ryle's view, and of Behaviourism generally. For Ryle the concept of mind is the concept of (certain sorts of) bodily behaviour. An alternative view, a better one I think, a view at least nearer to the truth, is that the concept of mind is the concept of the *inner cause*, or at least potential cause, of (certain sorts of) bodily behaviour. You can see easily enough how this view would fit an account of a purpose to get a drink from the fridge. We will come back to this point later on.

5.5. Ryle on dispositions

Behaviourism faces the obvious difficulty that mental states and such are not well correlated with behaviour. There can be perceptions, beliefs, thoughts, desires, and so on without any outward behaviour that expresses them. The extreme case here is *the totally paralyzed person*. This case can actually occur: In curare poisoning there can be total paralysis without loss of consciousness. For persons in that awful situation there can be willed action only within their own mind.

Ryle (who never himself mentions the case of total physical paralysis) proposes to get round this difficulty by introducing *dispositions* to behave (chap. 2, sec. 7; also chap. 5). 'Disposition' is a technical, important, and much used term in contemporary philosophy. It has no special connection with the mental. Paradigm dispositions are such things as brittleness and solubility. With dispositions we must distinguish sharply between the disposition and its *manifestation*. A manifestation of brittleness is breaking as a result of striking. The manifestation of solubility is dissolving as a result of being placed in liquid. Notice the *as a result of* clause in these two defini-

TABLE 5.1   An Analysis of Dispositions

Striking	plus	*Brittleness*	causes	*Breaking*
outer causal factor (*initiating cause*)		inner causal factor (*disposition*)		result (*manifestation*)

tions. To be a manifestation of a disposition the happening that is the manifestation of the disposition must be *caused* in a certain way.

A key feature of a disposition, and one that makes it suitable for Ryle's purposes, is that a thing can perfectly well have a disposition even when the disposition is not being manifested. Indeed, a thing can be brittle but never break, be soluble but never be dissolved. This feature of dispositions is then used to get over the difficulty of mental states and such in the absence of appropriate behaviour. Ryle says of this apparently difficult case for his position that the having of a certain disposition to behave in the absence of any *manifestation* of that disposition is enough. Quite a neat trick.

Notice that Ryle has to conceive of dispositions in a certain way. We can think of dispositions as actual states of the disposed thing. A manifestation of brittleness will then be a matter of the striking (we can call this the 'initiating cause') plus the inner state, together co-operating to cause the breaking. See Table 5.1.

This analysis of dispositions, though in itself plausible, is barred to Ryle because it treats the disposition itself as an inner cause, a cause that one originally hypothesizes only in virtue of its manifestation. One may then be able to go on to give a concrete description of it, for instance as a certain bonding of molecules for the case of brittleness. To treat a mental disposition in this way, though, is to go over to the inner cause model of the mental. This is just what Ryle is trying to get away from!

Instead, what Ryle says about dispositions is this:

> To possess a dispositional property is not to be in a particular state, or to undergo a particular change; it is to be bound or liable to be in a particular state, or undergo a particular change, when a particular condition is realized.

One can put it this way. Ryle is identifying the having of an unmanifested disposition (say, brittleness) with the truth of a *counterfactual* statement: "If O had been struck, then it would have broken." Counterfactuals, like dispositions, are much discussed in contemporary philosophy. (If you go back to the last two sections of Chapter 4—4.2.4 and 4.2.5—you will see that each is centrally concerned with counterfactuals.) They are hypothetical, 'if . . . then . . . ', statements, with the antecedent clause, the 'if' clause, false. Despite the falsity of the antecedent, such statements can often be true. It is true of a particular lump of sugar not put into water that if it had been put into water, it would have dissolved.

Now there is no doubt that statements that truly attribute dispositions to objects in the absence of a manifestation ('this—unstruck—glass is brittle') do regularly involve the truth of appropriate counterfactuals. But Ryle, as it were, leaves his counterfactuals hanging in the air. I mean by this that he seems to think that he does not have to say what it is in the world that makes these counterfactuals true. In place of unmanifested dispositions, he plugs in counterfactuals, but says nothing at all about what it is that makes these counterfactuals true.

We may call this purely counterfactual analysis of attributions of dispositions the 'Phenomenalist' theory of dispositions. It contrasts with the 'Realist' analysis just given above in Table 5.1, where dispositions are thought of as actual states of the disposed thing, states described causally in terms of their potential manifestations. But the question that Ryle should have faced, but never did, is what in the world makes his counterfactuals true. What is the ground in reality, what some philosophers nowadays call the *truthmaker*, for their truth? It would seem that an essential part of the truthmaker must be a suitable inner state of the disposed thing. But in that case, why not identify the disposition with the inner state? To follow out this line of thought, however, is to go over into that very inner cause picture that Ryle is trying to get away from. So it is blocked to him.

Notes

1. You can still find this argument around. See Cynthia MacDonald, "Weak Externalism and Mind–Body Identity," *Mind* 99 (1990): p. 391 n. 10.

Readings and references for Ryle

Armstrong, D. M. 1981. "Acting and Trying." In *The Nature of Mind and Other Essays*, pp. 68–88. Ithaca: Cornell University Press.

Kim, Jaegwon. 1996. *Philosophy of Mind*, Boulder, Colo.: Westview Press. Chapter 2, "Mind As Behavior: Behavorism", would be an excellent supplement to the present chapter.

Medlin, Brian. 1967. "Ryle and the Mechanical Hypothesis." In *The Identity Theory of Mind*, ed. C. F. Presley, pp. 94–150. St. Lucia: Queensland University Press.

_____. 1969. "Materialism and the Argument from Distinct Existences." In *The Business of Reason*, eds. J. J. MacIntosh and S. Coval, pp. 168–185. London: Routledge and Kegan Paul.

Melden, A. I. 1961. *Free Action*. London: Routledge and Kegan Paul.

Ryle, Gilbert. 1949. *The Concept of Mind*. London: Hutchinson.

Wittgenstein, Ludwig. 1953. *Philosophical Investigations*. Trans. G.E.M. Anscombe. Oxford: Blackwell.

Wood, Oscar P., and George Pitcher, eds. 1971. *Ryle*. London: Macmillan.

CHAPTER SIX

The Identity Theory

The texts for this chapter are U. T. Place, "Is Consciousness a Brain Process?" and J.J.C. Smart, "Sensations and Brain Processes".

The founding of the Identity theory is associated with the names of Place, Smart, and Herbert Feigl. Feigl's view is not quite the same as that of Place and Smart—it is not as hard-line in its materialism (though he gave us the useful phrase 'central-state materialism'). We will concentrate on Place and Smart. Place's pioneer article, "Is Consciousness a Brain Process?", was published in the *British Journal of Psychology* (1956), and so it did not get the same wide publicity among philosophers that Smart's "Sensations and Brain Processes" did three years later (*Philosophical Review*, 1959). Place and Smart were both in the Australian city of Adelaide in the 1950s (Place relatively briefly), and so they are often spoken of in philosophical circles as the founders of 'Australian Materialism'. But they were in fact British, though Smart is now an Australian.

6.1. Central-state Materialism revived

Place begins his article by indicating his sympathy with Physicalism. He cannot bring himself to accept the view, which we have seen in Descartes, Hume, and Huxley, that the mental is a distinct realm from the physical. Smart enlarges on this step of the argument. He says: "Science is increasingly giving us a viewpoint whereby organisms are able to be seen as physico-chemical mechanisms." Smart's words will remind us of Descartes and Huxley on the body. There is, says Smart, "Nothing in the world but increasingly complex arrangements of physical constituents." "Could consciousness be an exception?" he asks. In a phrase that Smart took over from Feigl, could sensations be 'nomological danglers'? ('Nomological' just means 'law-like', from the Greek 'nomos'.) You would need special laws relating simple constituents (the sensations) to complex physical configurations. But, he says:

> I cannot believe that ultimate laws of nature could relate simple constituents to configurations consisting of perhaps billions of neurons (and goodness knows how many billion billions of ultimate particles) all put together for all the world as though their main purpose in life was to be a negative feedback mechanism of a complicated sort. Such ultimate laws would be like nothing so far known in science.

(The last sentence should remind us of the Princess Elizabeth and her protest that Cartesian interactionism was like no other causal transaction that we are acquainted with.)

Back to Place. He sympathizes with Physicalism. But, he says, modern Physicalism is behaviouristic. He instances the psychologist Edward Tolman and the philosophers Wittgenstein and Ryle. Consciousness is thought of as a special type of behaviour, or else as a disposition to behave in a certain way. Having an itch, for instance, might be analyzed as a temporary propensity to scratch a portion of one's body.

And, indeed, Place says that he is prepared to accept a good deal of this view. For cognitive concepts such as knowing, believing, understanding, remembering, and for volitional concepts such as wanting and intending, such an analysis is 'fundamentally sound'. (Place said this over forty years ago, but would still say the same today. Not so with Smart, who went on after a few years to a more thoroughgoing central-state view.) However, says Place: "There would seem to be an intractable residue of concepts clustering around the notions of consciousness, experience, sensation, and mental imagery, where some sort of inner process story is unavoidable."

Are we then committed to Dualism? Must we say that "sensations and images form a separate category of processes over and above the physical and physiological processes with which they are known to be correlated?" At the time that Place wrote, a vast majority of analytical philosophers thought that an identification of sensations with physical brain processes could be quickly dismissed. Place sets out to advance an inner-mental-process Materialism by a *defensive* operation, by trying to show that it is an *intelligible and non-self-contradictory* thesis. If this thesis can be established, he thinks, then there are good scientific reasons—the sort of reasons we have just seen advanced by Smart—for thinking the thesis is true.

6.2. Finding a model

Consider the statement, "Consciousness is a brain process". Place tries to get clear about what sort of statement it is. He begins by distinguishing three sorts of 'is' statements, as shown in Table 6.1. The first thing he does is to get Group I out of the way.

If you look at examples (3) through to (7) you will see that for 'is' we could substitute 'is identical with'. All these statements are identity-statements. But to say that her hat is identical with redness or that giraffes are identical with tallness makes little sense. However, the hypothesis that consciousness is a brain process can very well be put by saying that consciousness is identical with a brain process. So Places' hypothesis belongs among (3) to (7). The linguistic test just given eliminates (1) and (2) as models for "Consciousness is a brain process". Place himself uses another test that gets the same result. He points out that for (3) to (7) you can add 'and nothing else' and make good sense. You can also say "Consciousness is a brain process and nothing else" and again make good sense. The 'and nothing else' just adds emphasis. But you can hardly say "Her hat is red and nothing else" or "Giraffes are tall and nothing else".

So now we want to know whether the statement "Consciousness is a brain process" is like the 'definitional' statements 3 and 4 in Group II or should be placed in Group III. Both sorts of statements are identity-statements, but otherwise they are different. At the time that Place was writing it would have been orthodox to classify the differences between Group II and Group III as indicated in Table 6.2.

Rehearsing these technical terms quickly: 'Analytic' means 'true solely in virtue of the meaning of the terms used'; a stock example is "A father is a male parent". 'Synthetic' just means 'not analytic'; for example, "San Francisco is north of Sydney". 'Known *a priori*' means 'known independently of experience', known purely by thought or calculation. The truths of mathematics and logic are

TABLE 6.1   Three Sorts of 'Is' Statement

I. *The 'is' of predication*	II. *The 'is' of definition*	III. *The 'is' of composition*
1. Her hat is red.	3. A square is an equilateral rectangle.	5. His table is an old packing case.
2. Giraffes are tall.	4. Red is a colour.	6. A cloud is a mass of water droplets or other particles in suspension.
		7. Lightning is an electric discharge.

generally held to be known *a priori*. To be 'known *a posteriori*' means 'to be known on the basis of experience'. It is known *a posteriori* that a day on earth is about twenty-four hours. Necessary truths are ones that cannot be denied without self-contradiction. Once again, the truths of mathematics and logic are generally held to be necessary. Contingent truths are truths that are not necessary. The truths of the empirical sciences are generally held to be contingent.

There was also a strong tendency when Place was writing to take 1–3 and 1a–3a as package deals, so that the three characteristics of the two groups went together or did not apply at all. Place shared this outlook. The situation is a bit more complicated today because of the influence of Saul Kripke, particularly with respect to 3 and 3a. Kripke thinks that there are truths that are synthetic (not true in virtue of meanings) and are also known *a posteriori* as a result of empirical research, but that are nevertheless necessary, thus breaking up the package deal. Furthermore, Kripke would certainly claim that the statements "Lightning is an electric discharge" and, I think, "A cloud is a mass of particles in suspension" are necessary truths, though obviously synthetic and known *a posteriori*. For Place, though, they are contingent.

We want to get away from these complications here, so let us just forget about 3 and 3a, which cause the complications. Statements in Group II, then, are analytic and known *a priori* (a plausible contention), whereas statements in Group III are synthetic and known

TABLE 6.2   Differences Between Group II and Group III Statements

(II)	(III)
1. analytic	1a. synthetic
2. known *a priori*	2a. known *a posteriori*
3. necessary	3a. contingent

a posteriori (clearly true). If we then consider the statement "Consciousness is a brain process" we can see clearly that it is synthetic. If true at all, it is certainly not true solely in virtue of the meanings of the words 'consciousness' and 'brain process'. And if true and knowable, it can be known only *a posteriori*, as a result of empirical research. So it goes into Group III.

Place argues, correctly I think, that the analytic philosophers of the day had rejected the idea that consciousness is a brain process because they were trying to force the claim into Group II. They could see that, judged by the standards of Group II, it had to be false. And they did judge it by those standards. (One English philosopher said of Place and Smart "A touch of the sun, I suppose". I have confirmed the story with that person!)

But why judge what is fairly obviously a Group III statement by Group II standards? This was due to the climate of analytic philosophy at that time. Influenced by Wittgenstein, by logical positivism, and by the Oxford 'ordinary language' philosophers, philosophers drew a sharp distinction between philosophy and science, a much sharper distinction than you would find today. Philosophy, if it issued in truth at all (Wittgenstein was doubtful), gave us nothing but conceptual truths, truths about the logico-semantic analysis of concepts. This meant that all philosophical truth had to be analytic and *a priori*, independent of scientific findings and empirical findings generally. At the same time, philosophers didn't give up interest in the mind–body problem (how could they?). So they kidded themselves that the problem could be solved by *a priori* conceptual analysis. (I plead guilty myself, before hearing Smart read the "Sensations and Brain processes" paper at Melbourne University some time before it was published in 1959.)

Place, however, saw that, true or false, "Consciousness is a brain process" is a Group III statement. It is an empirical identity claim. So is it like "His table is an old packing case"? No, because that statement is "a particular proposition which refers to a particular case". What then of "A cloud is a mass of particles in suspension"? That is getting a bit warmer. But it is still unsatisfactory because the statement about the cloud is one that can be directly verified by the senses. You can get inside an atmospheric cloud and experience the moisture. True, consciousness can be observed, at least in our own case. And brain processes can be observed, to a small degree at least, although the observation is rather 'theory-laden'. But it is a purely theoretical step to identify our introspectively observed sensations with certain of our brain processes. In this respect, then, the identification is like the identification of lightning with an electrical discharge. Observed lightning is, on the basis of a theory, identified with the postulated electricity. So Place takes statement 7, "Lightning is an electric discharge", as his model for sensation/brain process identity.

Why should we *identify* conscious processes with brain processes? Why not simply treat them as *well-correlated* phenomena like the stages of the moon that are correlated with the movements of the tide? This objection was often raised at the beginning against the Identity theory. Place's answer is not particularly clear. Smart said the following, and what he said became orthodoxy among those who were attracted to the Identity theory:

> If it be agreed that there are no cogent philosophical arguments which force us into accepting dualism, and if the brain process theory and dualism are equally consistent with the facts, then the principles of parsimony and simplicity seem to me to decide overwhelmingly in favour of the brain process theory.

6.3. The 'phenomenological fallacy'

Place considers one important objection to his view. It is really a new application of the Properties argument (different properties, so different things), and I will present it as such. Suppose that somebody has a green after-image. (You can get one by looking intently at a red surface for a while, and then transferring your gaze to some white surface. A portion of the white surface will look to be more or less green.) Suppose also that the occurrence of the after-image is well correlated with the occurrence of a certain process in that person's brain (in the 'visual cortex'). Is this mere correlation or is it identity? It is not identity, it is argued, because:

1. The after-image is green.
2. The brain process is not (or need not be) green.

So the after-image cannot be identical with the brain process.

Place replies to this by saying that, strictly, there are no such things as after-images, there is only the having of after-images. (We might write it as the-having-of-after-images.) Having a green after-image, he says, does not involve the having-of-something-green. So, he says, the objection fails.

A similar line had already been taken by Ryle in his discussion of mental images in *The Concept of Mind*. After-images are not the same as mental images because after-images are a species of illusory visual sense-impression or sensation, whereas mental images are associated with remembering and imagining. But Ryle's point can be applied to after-images as well as mental images. What Ryle said was that there were no such things as mental images but only a process of imaging, a process that might be, or might not be, under control of the will. He would certainly have gone on to deny that imaging something green involved having something green. If we ignore the fact that Ryle wants then to 'behaviourize' imaging (a most unpromising pro-gramme!), we can take him to be making the same point as Place.

But if we take the Place/Ryle line, what do we mean when we say that we are having a green after-image? Place says, "When we de-scribe the after-image as green, we are not saying that there is some-thing, the after-image, that is green; we are saying we are having the sort of experience which we normally have when, and which we have learned to describe as, looking at a green patch of light." It is the *experience* that is to be identified with a brain process. I believe that this reply is correct as far as it goes, but it is easy to think that Place (and Ryle) have pushed off the difficulty by a merely verbal manoeuvre.

Here is what may be a deeper, though controversial, reply to the objection Place is seeking to answer. To have an after-image is not to have something green in one's mind. Rather it is to have in one's mind a *representation* of something green. It is an illusory and rather temporary representation that, say, a certain white wall has a greenish patch in the middle of the white-painted surface. One attractive feature of this analysis of the situation is that we have an incurable tendency not to distinguish clearly between representations and what they represent. Children do this spontaneously from the earliest age. A picture of a wolf *is* a wolf. The shapes on a photograph *are* your mother and father. In the same way, perhaps, we mistakenly think that having an after-image *is* having something green. But really it is only the representation of something green.

This suggestion may be thought to involve a fairly obvious difficulty. Representations demand a *medium* of representation. The medium may be expanses of paint on canvas; it may be marks on paper; it may be sounds issuing from mouths; and so on. But there seems to be no medium of representation in the case of having an after-image. To this objection, however, there is also a fairly obvious reply. The reply agrees that there has to *be* some medium of representation but then suggests that we could well lack any direct acquaintance with the nature of the medium. The medium of representation might be modifications of, encodings in, something immaterial. Or it might be modifications of, encodings in, something material. But our introspective awareness of having an after-image fails to answer this question. If it did, the mind–body problem would be a bit easier!

6.4. The secondary qualities

But there is one problem with what Place says that should perhaps be introduced immediately. In developing his account of what it is to have a green after-image, Place emphasizes that the word 'green' is a public word. It is applied to a public property of public objects. It is a property of leaves while they are still on trees, of grass before it gets too dry, of the skin of Granny Smith apples. This claim actually creates a problem for Materialist or Physicalist metaphysics.

The trouble is that the colours belong to a group of properties—other members being felt heat and cold, sounds, smells and tastes—that since the time of John Locke have been called the secondary qualities. They are contrasted with such properties as shape, size, motion, and mass, which Locke called the primary qualities. (He took the terms from Robert Boyle. The contrast between the two sorts of property is already to be found in Galileo.) The secondary qualities were given that name because they seem to play no part in 'the executive order of nature', a nice phrase we owe to the philosopher-psychologist G. F. Stout. The only properties that the physicist seems to need in the quest to give an account of the workings of the physical world are the primary properties.

What to do with the secondary qualities then? The obvious thing to do seems to be to treat them as something 'subjective'. Put them in that well-known philosophical dustbin (trash can in the United States): the mind. Locke says that greenness in objects is a mere power to cause green 'ideas' (sensations) in us. That special quality of greenness that all those who have our sort of colour vision are acquainted with, he seems to attribute to the 'ideas'.

But once one seeks to extend Materialism to the mind, as Place seeks to do, this policy about the secondary qualities, which seemed a good idea at the time, becomes an embarrassment. In the course of giving an account of what it is to have a green after-image Place insists that 'green' is a public word, ascribing a public quality to public objects. But this quality, it seems, is not wanted in the physical world, at any rate if we are seeking a scientific worldview.

Place does not discuss the problem. Smart does pay it some attention in "Sensations and Brain Processes" (see Objection 3, par. 2–4). Unfortunately, his solution to the problem, a solution he repeated in his important book *Philosophy and Scientific Realism*, seems much too behaviouristic. My own, quite controversial, view is that what is required is an Identity theory for the secondary qualities, a theory in which they are identified with certain microphysical properties of physical bodies, for instance, felt heat with motions of molecules. The detail of such identifications is still scientifically tricky in the extreme. But on this view the secondary qualities will turn out after all to be part, though a rather insignificant part, of the executive order of nature. They will not, however, be something additional to the primary qualities. More recently, Smart has come round to the same sort of view. (See the section on colours in his 1989 book, *Our Place in the Universe*, chap. 5. I will say more on the puzzling secondary qualities later, in Chapter 11.)

6.5. Smart and topic neutrality

Perhaps the most important thing that Smart did in "Sensations and Brain Processes" was to further develop Place's answer to the Properties argument. We will get to this answer by considering Smart's reply to Objection 3, which he says is the most subtle and difficult to meet, in his article. The model he is using to understand the sensation/brain-process identity is the true statement "The Morning Star is the Evening Star". Although this statement is about an individual entity, the planet Venus, it clearly belongs in Place's Group III: It is synthetic and known *a posteriori*. Incidentally, it clearly seems to be contingent.

Figure 6.1 is a diagram of the situation. Notice that the two phrases at the bottom have been set in quotation marks to symbolize that this is a diagram of a *semantic* situation: the way that two verbal descriptions hook on to the one object, a planet. Although the Morning Star is identical with, is the very same thing as, the Evening Star, the two phrases—in the philosophical jargon introduced by Bertrand Russell they are 'definite descriptions'—pick out Venus via two distinct properties. Correlated with the two phrases (the two predicates, as philosophers say) are two perfectly objective, if rather complex, properties. These properties are distinct from each other, in the sense that having one of them fails to entail having the other. These are the properties *being the Morning Star* and *being the Evening Star*. Venus has both properties. (They are rather complicated properties: the Morning Star is the last star to vanish from the sky in the morning at certain times of year; the Evening Star is the first star to appear in the evening at certain times of year. The Greeks, and perhaps earlier peoples, came to realize that they were one and the same object.)

Now consider the statement, "Having an after-image is having a certain sort of brain process". Figure 6.2 is a diagram of the semantic situation. By analogy with the Venus case, the two predicates will pick out the same thing via different properties. The right-hand predicate is no problem. The properties that make a thing a brain process are purely physical properties. *But in virtue of what property(ies) does the predicate 'having an after-image' apply?* Will not that property have to be something non-physical? So we are back at Dualism again. This is Objection 3.

The first point that Smart makes is that the objection (which he says came from Max Black) does not necessarily lead to a substance-Dualism. It might involve only a weaker *property-Dualism*. It might lead only to what is called a 'Dual-attribute' theory. The brain could

FIGURE 6.1   Semantic Picture I

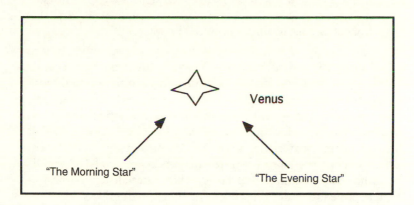

FIGURE 6.2   Semantic Picture II

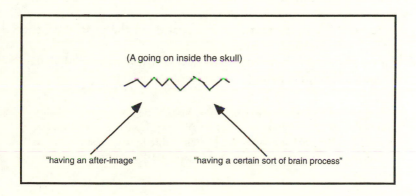

be thought of as a substance bearing two quite different sorts of properties: properties that are purely physical, and mental properties such as after-imaging. But, as Smart indicates, for a Materialist such a view is just about as bad as full blown Dualism.

Smart's second point contains his important contribution. It is an improved version of Place's answer. Smart says:

> "I see a yellowish-orange" after-image means (roughly) *"There is*
> *something going on which is like what is going on when* I have my
> eyes open, am awake, and there is an orange illuminated in good light
> in front of me, that is, when I really see an orange."

Smart emphasizes that the words italicized involve only quasi-logi-
cal, topic neutral words. (The useful phrase 'topic neutral' comes
from Ryle.) The report about the after-image is abstract, saying
nothing about the intrinsic (non-relational) properties of the mental
process. The report is therefore *neutral* between Dualism, Dual-
attribute, and Materialist theories of the nature of the mental
process. The possibility of Materialism is therefore left open. The
scientific considerations that favour the Materialist hypothesis are
then appealed to in deciding the issue between the rivals.

Smart illustrates the topic neutral nature of the analysis by comparing:

1. The dentist called.
2. The doctor called.
3. Someone called.

Number 3 is topic neutral and leaves open the possibility that
number 1 or number 2 is true.

It is important to notice the critical role that the word 'like' plays
in Smart's formula. He says:

> The strength of my reply depends upon the possibility of our being
> able to report that one thing is like another [having an after-image,
> actually seeing an orange] without being able to state the respect in
> which it is like [some actual neurophysiological likeness, if the brain-
> process is correct].

Smart does not think that this is a problem:

> If we think cybernetically about the nervous system we can envisage
> it as being able to respond to certain likenesses of its internal
> processes without being able to do more. It would be easier to build a
> machine which would tell us, say on a punched tape, whether or not

two objects were similar, than it would be to build a machine which would report wherein the similarities consisted.

With this reply, Smart thinks he has answered the most outstanding difficulty for the Place/Smart Identity theory. But Kim Sterelny has pointed out to me that Smart might also have appealed to all sorts of everyday examples where similarities (and differences) are perceived without our being able to pick up respects of similarity (or difference). That speakers of, say, English 'have the same accent' is something that speakers of that language who have a good ear can fairly reliably detect. Yet only a trained phonologist can give an account of what that similarity consists in. Face recognition, wine recognition, and a host of other perceptual skills are also like this. Smart is suggesting that the introspective awareness of the likeness between after-imaging and actually seeing is a similar, though still more radical, awareness of similarity without awareness of the respect of similarity.

Smart's explicit recognition of the topic neutrality fundamentally involved in our mental concepts was, in my view, his major contribution to the working out of the Identity theory, and, more generally, to contemporary Materialism about the mind. Our mind is not experienced by us as immaterial or material. What its true nature is, is a matter of theory. This insight is available for theories that differ from Smart in all sorts of detail. Suppose, for instance, that we give an account of what it is to have a yellowish-orange after-image as a *representation* of a yellowish-orange object in the world. We can still maintain a topic neutral thesis that we have no direct insight into the medium in which this representation is encoded. As with Smart's analysis, this claim leaves open the possibility that the representation is no more than a physical encoding in a purely material brain.

6.6. Mind–body interaction

Descartes and Hume, we saw, allowed that mental states and processes could act on the body, in particular to produce behaviour. It is a natural and obvious view, just commonsense, really. But since they thought that the mind was non-physical, they had to say that in such action the non-physical acted on the physical. Commentator after commentator, from the Princess Elizabeth onwards, suggested that this was hard to understand. We have no clear model in our other experience, they said, for causal action of this special sort.

Notice how the Identity theory sweeps such difficulties aside. Your desire to have something to drink causes you to go to the fridge to get out a bottle of beer. On the Identity view, your purpose is (is identical with) a material process in your brain. This material process causes your body to behave in this appropriate way. Material happening causes material happening. The material happening in your brain is a particularly complex and sophisticated sort of cause, which we are still only just beginning to understand. But the causation is ordinary physical causation.

Readings and references for the Identity theory

Borst, C. V., ed. 1970. *The Mind–Brain Identity Theory*. London: Macmillan.

Feigl, H. *The "Mental" and the "Physical": The Essay and a Postscript*. 1967. Minneapolis: University of Minnesota Press.

Place, U. T. 1956. "Is Consciousness a Brain Process?" *British Journal of Psychology* 47: pp. 44–50. Reprinted in William G. Lycan, *Mind and Cognition*. Cambridge, Mass:. Blackwell, 1990; and in many other places

Smart, J.J.C. 1959. "Sensations and brain processes." *Philosophical Review* 68: pp.141–156. Reprinted often.

_____. 1989. *Our Place in the Universe: A Metaphysical Discussion*. Oxford: Blackwell.

CHAPTER SEVEN

The Causal Theory— Armstrong and Lewis

The texts for this chapter are Armstrong's A Materialist Theory of the Mind, *chapter 6, and Lewis's "An Argument for the Identity Theory".*

The work of Armstrong and Lewis follows rather directly upon that of Place and Smart. Both Armstrong and Lewis try to meet difficulties in, and develop the position of, Place and Smart. They are often classified as Identity theorists, and this classification is correct enough, but they both put special emphasis upon causality in their account, and it is convenient to call their sort of view the Causal theory. It could also be called Causal Functionalism.

Armstrong's starting idea (emphasized by Lewis only in his second paper) was that the restriction of the Identity theory to sensations, images, and consciousness was ill-conceived. (This point was fairly soon accepted by Smart, but never by Place.) Armstrong thought that it was not a theoretical economy to give quite different accounts of different sorts of mental phenomena. It appeared to him that a *central-state* account of beliefs, desires, and so on is as desirable as a central-state account the having of after-images.

Armstrong was impressed both by Objection 3, which he thought was the one to answer, and also by Smart's reply to it by means of a topic neutral analysis. But it seemed clear that Smart's formula would have to be revised. Although Smart did not bring out the point clearly, his topic neutral analysis was a *causal* one.

(English-speaking empiricists have had difficulty in focussing on causation, except when causation itself was the direct object of study. This was the result of the influence of Hume and his utterly deflationary doctrine that causation is nothing but regular succession. It made causation seem rather unimportant in philosophical analyses. The situation is only now beginning to be remedied.) Smart should have said: What is going on in me is like what goes on when an orange *acts* on me (acts on my eyes). What goes on is the *effect* of a certain sort of cause. Psychologists speak of such a cause as a *stimulus*. The orange is the *distal* stimulus, and the effect on the retina is the *proximal* stimulus. All this is causal language.

But suppose we want to generalize the Place/Smart account to all mental events, processes, and states. Suppose we want a central-state account of them all. The Place/Smart account of inner mental episodes was given in terms of certain sorts of causes, certain sorts of stimuli. But it does not seem possible to give an analysis of thoughts, beliefs, purposes, and intentions in terms of their causes. They have causes, of course, like anything else. But their causes cannot be part of their definition.

Perhaps, however, beliefs, purposes, and so on can be defined as the inner cause (topic neutrally described, of course) of certain sorts of effect. What sorts of effect? The obvious candidate is *behaviour*. What is a current purpose to get a drink? It is an inner cause that has initiated, and is sustaining, behaviour tending to bring about drinking by the one who has the purpose. That looks like at least a good beginning of saying what a purpose is.

This beginning led Armstrong up to two formulae. Mental states and such are:

1. States *apt* for the producing of (causing of) certain ranges of behaviour.
2. States *apt* for being produced by (caused by) certain ranges of causes.

The second formula was a descendant of the Smart formula for the having of an after-image. The Smart formula was meant to serve only some mental states, perceptions, bodily sensations, and so on. Armstrong retained this restriction: formula 2 was *not* meant to apply to purposes, beliefs, and so on. But formula 1 was the really vital formula.

In the new scheme, therefore, perceptions, after-images, and so on were supposed to fall under (1) as well as under (2); that is to say, besides being states apt for being produced in a certain way, they are also to be thought of as states apt for producing. In particular, perceptions are states that give a *capacity* for reaction back onto the world. This capacity is a capacity for selective behaviour, *discriminatory* behaviour. Without perception, the organism cannot operate in its environment, and for Armstrong this capacity to so operate is an essential component of perception. The capacity may not, for one reason or another, be *used*. But it must be there.

7.1. Dispositions once more

All this makes us think about Ryle's dispositions again. Ryle thought that to have a certain belief, for instance, is to have a disposition to behave in a certain way, with the behaviour, if it occurs, as the manifestation of that belief. (Ryle had to face the fact that, unlike paradigm dispositions, such as brittleness, the behaviour in which a particular belief is manifested could be of many different sorts. He tried to get over this with a quite ingenious idea. Unlike *single-track* dispositions, such as brittleness and solubility, belief that the earth is round is a *multi-track* disposition. It has many different possible manifestations.)

As we have seen, for Ryle dispositions do not name inner causes (described after their effects: their manifestations). Ryle has a 'Phenomenalist' theory of dispositions. For a thing or a person to have a certain disposition is just the conditional truth that, in certain situations, the thing or person will behave in certain ways. But suppose we move to a Realist theory of dispositions. Suppose we think of a disposition as an inner cause, topic neutrally described by what it plays a part in bringing about. Then we can say that the dispositional theory of belief is at least getting warm.

In general, although the mind should not be identified with behaviour, it is much nearer the truth to identify it with dispositions to behave, with the dispositions conceived as inner causes.

7.2. Lewis and causal role

Armstrong's formulae are too *atomistic*. They give the impression that mental states and such should be defined one by one. But in fact behaviour, in particular, depends upon a whole battery of mental states. For instance, perception of P involves selective behaviour involving P only if we decide to engage in such behaviour. And the decision so to engage may be the resultant of all sorts of desires and calculations.

Lewis produced a most useful broadening, that was also a simplifying, formulation. He said that mental states, processes, and events are defined by their *causal role*. This causal role involves not merely external causes apt for producing mental states, and the behaviour that mental states are apt for producing, but also, and importantly, the causal relations that mental states within the one mind bear to one another.

In so widening the scope of the formula, Lewis brought out something important: the *package-deal* nature of the mental concepts. Package-deal concepts are a familiar enough phenomenon: Consider the simple examples of husband/wife and soldier/army. No husband without a wife, no wife without a husband; no soldier without an army, no army without soldiers. Such package-deal concepts *apply together or not at all*. Mental concepts are characteristically package-deal concepts, and the packages are the most complex and sophisticated ones that we find among our everyday concepts. (This is not surprising, because the mind is the most complex and sophisticated thing that we know to exist. Sophisticated concepts are needed for a sophisticated thing.)

I am inclined to think that there is one great central package involved in the notion of mentality. The parts of the package are the notions of purpose, perception, and belief. Here purpose is the first half of the package. It seems that purpose involves perception and, at least for the higher mammals, belief. The second half of the package is perception and belief; they involve purposes.

1. *Purposes involve perception and belief.* Let us consider not so much purposes but the products, the effects, of purposes: actual purposive activity. Take some simple activity like getting a beer from the fridge. It is really quite a complex affair. One has to navigate all the way to the fridge and then take appropriate action. There is no way that this long train of actions can be carried out except by a continuous perception of the developing situation, ending with the perception that the goal has been achieved. Perception has to keep the action on course every step of the way. Action may have to be

modified because perception makes one aware of unexpected obstacles: say, the fridge door being unexpectedly difficult to open. No end of knowledge and belief must feed into the purpose for there to be such purposive activity, for instance, knowledge where the kitchen is, what the fridge looks like, not to mention what a bottle of beer looks like, and how you get access to the beer inside the bottle.

Perhaps in the case of simple organisms action is controlled by perception alone, without belief. But in any case, purposes, unsophisticated or sophisticated, may be said to be *information-sensitive* causes. It is of the essence of purposes that they get carried out by what information theorists call negative feedback, information (or misinformation) that feeds into the purpose, modifying it in such a way that, if all goes well, the purpose is achieved. So it seems plausible to say that purposive activity entails perception and, with reasonably sophisticated creatures, belief.

2. Perception and belief involve purpose. Now to argue for the less obvious connection, the link going from perceptions and beliefs to purposes. When a purpose issues in purposive activity, perceptions and beliefs about the developing situation are automatically involved. But it is perfectly possible, and regularly occurs, that we have current perceptions and beliefs that are completely irrelevant to our current purposive activity. What we can say, however, is that perceptions and beliefs are always *potentially relevant* to the carrying out of a purpose. You perceive that the light has turned green. If you are not driving a car, or not interested in crossing the road as a pedestrian, the green light may not affect your conduct at all. But the information is potentially relevant. If you had been driving or trying to cross the road, then the information might well have affected your conduct. Perceptions and beliefs are states that must have that sort of relevance to your conduct: relevance in suitable circumstances.

One way that this point can be brought out is by considering the difference between a proposition that you really believe and the same proposition that you merely 'entertain' without giving it any belief. It is easy enough to entertain the thought that the sun will not rise tomorrow. Philosophers who think about the problem of induction spend quite a portion of their lives entertaining this thought. But they do not believe it. If they really believed it, or even if they thought there was a real chance of it, they would factor it into all sorts of deliberations and actions. That, I think, is a conceptual point about thoughts that do not involve belief. They are not potentially relevant to conduct in the way that they would have been relevant if they had been beliefs.

7.3. A new model: gene = DNA molecule

Place used as his model statement "Lightning is an electric discharge", and he said that the 'is' here is the 'is' of composition. Sensations are composed of, are constituted by, brain processes. The composition point seems fine, but his statement model fails to capture the point about causal role. Brian Medlin (another important 'Australian Materialist') made the excellent suggestion that the statement "The gene is the DNA molecule" is the sort of model that the Causal theory requires. The concept of the gene is:

1. causal
2. topic neutral
3. theoretical

Causal. Complex patterns of characteristics are observed in closely related organisms, especially in those organisms that are related as ancestor to close descendant. A causal link is hypothesized, mediated by entities called genes. A person's genes are apt for being caused by ancestral genes and are apt to bring about (cause) certain characteristics in descendants. Just as in the mental case, it is generally genes acting in complex combinations, and not atomistically, that produce the hereditary characteristics.

Topic neutral. In early genetic theory nothing was known of the intrinsic nature of the genes. They were described in a purely topic neutral way as factors that play a certain causal role. It is only relatively recently that their concrete nature, their *composition*, has been discovered: that they are segments of DNA at the centre of cells.

Theoretical. Here there is a difference between genes and the mental case, but one easily discounted for. Genes began as purely theoretical postulations. But, with respect to some of our own mental processes and states, we have a direct cognitive access. We are conscious of them. We will talk about the nature of consciousness in Chapter 10. In any event, this difference hardly detracts at all from the helpfulness of Medlin's model.

7.4. Some fine tuning

On the Causal theory, then, the identification of mental processes and states with brain processes and states involves two clearly separate steps:

(1) A conceptual analysis of the various sorts of mental concepts, including their interlocking. Result: a topic neutral account, with mental processes and states defined in terms of their causal role.
(2) A (contingent) identification of these processes and states with processes and states in the brain (in the central nervous system). This is defended as the best hypothesis available, given the scientific evidence.

It may be noted that Armstrong and Lewis understand the first, conceptual, step a bit differently. Lewis writes:

> Our view is that the concept of pain, or indeed any other experience or mental state, is the concept of a state that occupies a certain causal role, a state with certain typical causes and effects. It is the concept of a state apt for being caused by certain stimuli and apt for causing certain behaviour. Or, better, of a state apt for being caused in certain ways by stimuli plus other mental states and apt for combining with certain other mental states to jointly cause certain behaviour. It is the concept of a system of states that together more or less realize the pattern of causal generalizations set forth in commonsense psychology. ("Mad Pain and Martian Pain")

It is the last sentence *only* that Armstrong finds doubtful. Lewis's idea is that we build into our mental concepts basic causal generalizations about mental states, for instance, the sorts of things that pains make us do, such as wincing and groaning. But it is unclear whether such things are really part of our *concept* of pain. Pain (physical pain) is a bodily sensation (bodily perception) of a particular sort. It is the bodily sensation that, in general, we dislike having more than any other. (The word 'pain' derives from the Latin *poena*, meaning 'punishment'.) Whether our concept of pain takes us further is doubtful. Pain might not have caused groaning, but rather the facial movements of smiling. Yet it would not have been any the less painful. Groaning, crying out, and so on seem to be, evolutionarily speaking, devices for getting assistance, or even attempts to set up counter-irritants that will in some degree distract us from the pain. They do not seem to be part of the essence of pain.

A final note. Some contemporary philosophers seek to finesse this whole dispute about the concepts of mental processes and states by denying that step 1, the causal step in the Causal theorist's argument, is a conceptual step at all. According to Michael Levin, all we have in the so-called conceptual step are *identifying descriptions* (what Russell called 'definite descriptions') of mental processes and states. Levin also calls them 'Australian descriptions'. They do not give the essence of the mental. 'The Morning star' and 'the Evening star' are identifying descriptions, the first such descriptions we had of the planet Venus. They were the first ways that we had of identifying that object. But it is not a conceptual truth that Venus answers to these descriptions. It is not part of Venus's essence. (See Levin, *Metaphysics and the Mind–Body Problem*.)

If this contention of Levin's is correct, the Causal theory is not refuted, but its logical status is changed. It changes from being a scheme for the logical analysis of the mental concepts to an empirical theory as to how the mental happens to work.

Readings and references for the Causal theory

Armstrong, D. M. 1980. *The Nature of Mind*. Ithaca: Cornell University Press.

_____. 1993. *A Materialist Theory of the Mind*. Paperback ed., with a new preface. London: Routledge. See chapter 6 especially.

Armstrong, D. M., and Norman Malcolm. 1984. *Consciousness and Causality*. Oxford: Blackwell. Armstrong here debates the nature of mind with a prominent Wittgensteinian philosopher.

Levin, Michael. 1979. *Metaphysics and the Mind–Body Problem*. Oxford: Clarendon Press. See chapter 4, section 5.

Lewis, David. 1966. "An Argument for the Identity Theory." *Journal of Philosophy* 63: pp. 17–25. Reprinted as Chap. 7 in *Philosophical Papers*. Vol. 1. New York: Oxford University Press, 1983.

_____. 1972. "Psychophysical and Theoretical Identifications." *Australasian Journal of Philosophy* 50: pp. 249–258. More difficult than the paper of Lewis's just cited, but has been very influential.

_____. 1980. "Mad Pain and Martian Pain." In *Readings in the Philosophy of Psychology*. Vol. 1, ed. Ned Block, pp. 216–222. Reprinted, with a new postscript, as Chap. 9 in *Philosophical Papers*. Vol.1. New York: Oxford University Press, 1983.

CHAPTER EIGHT

The Eliminativist Theory

For texts see David Rosenthal, The Nature of Mind, *sec. III D; and* W. G. Lycan, Mind and Cognition, *sec. IV.*

The Eliminativist theory of the mind, we could also call it the Disappearance theory, was first put forward by Paul Feyerabend and Richard Rorty. Nowadays it is upheld particularly by Paul and Patricia Churchland. Go back to the Properties argument (different properties → different things) that Descartes and Hume used against any Materialist identification of mind and brain. Place and Smart wrestled with the Properties argument. Smart considered the objection that the after-image is yellowish-orange, or that the pain is throbbing and intense, but the corresponding brain process is not yellowish orange, or was not throbbing and intense. His topic neutral translations of statements about havings-of-after-images and havings-of-throbbing-pains ("something is going on in me like . . . ") was meant to meet this objection.

In a 1970 article ("Incorrigibility As a Mark of the Mental") Rorty makes various objections to the topic neutral translation thesis found in Smart and carried on by Armstrong and Lewis. One objection is that the alleged translations do not really work as translations. That objection, if well-founded, could be met by claiming that the so-called translations are no more than what Michael Levin called 'identifying descriptions' of mental processes and states, descriptions that are only *contingently* true. Rorty's second objection is that, given a topic neutral account, we can't even understand the Dualist theory. Smart thought that he had provided for the possibility that Materialism is false by leaving the blank in his formula. But really all he had provided for was the possibility that the mental is *non-physical*, a provision that, Rorty claims, does not do justice to Dualism. Rorty, however, places the greatest weight on his third objection: "It is part of the sense of 'mental' that being mental is incompatible with being physical."

This is pretty much what Descartes and Hume would have said. Suppose we grant the point. In that case, isn't Materialism as it applies to human beings and higher animals completely defeated? Rorty says, "No". There is a way out: Solve the problem for the Materialist by denying that there are such things as sensations and minds. There are only brain processes and brains.

Before going on to consider the model that Rorty proposes for his view, we may note that later Eliminativists, such as Paul and Patricia Churchland, place no particular emphasis on the point that the mental is supposed to be non-physical. Their idea is just that 'folk psychology' is a hopelessly unsatisfactory theory. It needs to be replaced by a scientific neurophysiology, and the new theory has no need to make reference to anything mental. I think the Churchland's Eliminativism faces much the same difficulties as those I will try to identify in Rorty's position.

8.1. Rorty's model

As we might expect, Rorty offers models for his brand of Materialism. In the past it was falsely asserted that:

(1)   Heat is caloric fluid.

and that

(2)   Certain unhappy and disturbed old women are witches.

These statements are both untrue, because heat turned out not to be any sort of fluid, and nobody can ride in the air on a broomstick. But here are two statements that *are* true:

(1*) Heat is the phenomenon that was once *thought* to be caloric fluid.

(2*) Certain unhappy and disturbed old women were once *thought* to be witches.

In the same way, Rorty claims, it is false that:

(3) Sensations are brain processes.

but it is true that:

(3*) The things we *thought* were sensations are really only brain processes.

Materialism is true because sensations, which would refute materialism if they existed, do not in fact exist.[1]

There is one peculiar feature of Rorty's models (heat/caloric fluid, disturbed old women/witches) that should be noted. They seem to depend upon the very 'theory'—the theory that mental entities exist—that Rorty is trying to cast doubt upon. People, he says, *falsely believed* that heat was caloric fluid, that certain old women were witches. He says, again, that the existence of the mental is, or is likely to be, a mere myth to which we all subscribe. But to speak of false belief and myths is to speak the language of mentality.

Quite unlike the models of caloric fluid and witches, the existence of the mental is such a deeply embedded assumption in our thinking that it is not at all easy to see what language is available to us in which it can be denied. Notice that the last sentence was not written in a 'neutral' style; in talking about our 'thinking', it itself presupposed the existence of the mental. For myself, I do not know how to present Rorty's thesis neutrally. Does Rorty? He appears to be sawing away at a branch on which he, along with the rest of us, is sitting. And it is a branch that neither he nor we know how to move from.

8.2. Comparison with the Free Will debate

It may help to see Eliminativism in perspective if we compare the mind–body debate with the Free Will problem. According to *Com-*

patibilism (Soft Determinism), the existence of free will is logically compatible with the Deterministic thesis (which may or may not be true) that everything is subject to deterministic causation. (According to Compatibilists, we are free when we can *choose* what to do, or, perhaps, when we can choose what to do and are not in a situation of coercion. Choosing, they say, is an empirical phenomenon and does not cease to be choosing because it has determining causes.) The parallel theory in the mind–body discussion is that the existence of mental processes is compatible with the truth of physicalism: that every natural process is a physical process. From this point of view, both Identity theorists and Causal theorists are Compatibilists about the mind–body problem.

In the Free Will debate, however, there are philosophers who reject Compatibilism. Their basic contention is that free will exists only if Determinism is false. The falsity of Determinism is a necessary condition of freedom. But given this basic incompatibility, there are then two different ways for Incompatibilists to jump. They can say that free will exists and *therefore* Determinism is false. This is the *Libertarian* position. But some Incompatibilists have argued that Determinism is true and that *therefore* there is no free will. This is the *Hard Determinist* view. So you get three basic positions on the Free Will problem. Note that we are in no way here wishing to argue about the three positions. We just want to compare them with positions about the mind–body problem.

Turning back to that problem, we find that there are Incompatibilists here also. An Incompatibilist will argue that if everything is material (physical), then the mind cannot exist (or at least is an outmoded theory, given present neurological theory). If you combine this with the acceptance that the mental exists, then you will be a Dualist. But the comparison with the Free Will problem shows us that there is another way for an Incompatibilist to go, parallel to Hard Determinism. You can argue that everything is physical and therefore that the mental does not exist. You are then an Eliminativist. See Figure 8.1 for the parallels.

This little taxonomy (classification) brings out the *double-edged* nature of Eliminativism. It shares an incompatibility with Dualism and is thus exposed to Dualist counter-attack. The Eliminativist has got round the Properties problem. It does not matter for an Eliminativist that the mental has different properties from the physical.

FIGURE 8.1   Free Will and Mind–Body Problems

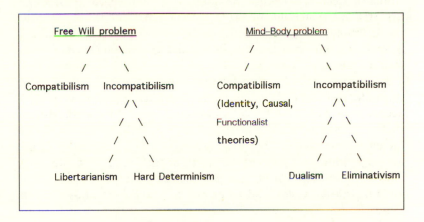

Hence Eliminative Materialism does not have to be backed up by the topic neutral manoeuvre. But Eliminativists make themselves vulnerable to Dualist criticism in another way. Dualists can and do argue against the Eliminativist that the mind is real, that we are directly aware of mental goings-on, that it is a fact of observation that we have pains, thoughts, and so on. All this, the Dualist will go on to say, is much more certain than the relatively speculative view that human beings are wholly physical beings. So, the Dualist will argue, the Eliminativist ought to turn Dualist.

It is, by the way, an interesting exercise for Compatibilists to consider what they would think if they became persuaded that Incompatibilism is the true position with regard to the mind–body problem. My own position is Compatibilist. But if persuaded (say by an Eliminativist) that Incompatibilism is true, I would then (reluctantly) turn Dualist, because the existence of the mental seems to me to be pretty well undeniable.

8.3. Why did Eliminativism arise?

Why has it taken so long for Eliminativism to emerge? There were Dualists in classical Greece, notably Plato in the *Phaedo*. There were also Materialists. The Greek Atomists (Leucippus and Democritus) thought that the mind consisted of swift, smooth, round, hot atoms that coursed around the body with great speed. (Not a bad first stab at a Materialist theory!) But as far as I know, nobody held the Eliminativist theory until thirty years ago. Why, to take a metaphor from evolutionary theory, did this ecological niche remain unfilled for so long?

The answer, I think, lies in the recent questioning of the old, once unchallenged distinction between observation and theory. The deeper *nature* of mind has always been difficult to discern. But to challenge its existence seems to be setting oneself up against one of the most obvious deliverances of experience. Descartes, we remember, even found his *primary certainty* in the existence of his own mind. That became an orthodox view: the existence of one's own mental processes was held to be the first and best known of all things.

Kim Sterelny has asked why Hard Determinism is not also an unfilled niche. Is not our freedom to choose as introspectively obvious to us as the existence of our mental processes? But I do not think that the parallel holds. Suppose we are deliberating what to do in some situation where, as we would naturally describe it, we are 'free to choose'. What the Hard Determinist says is that the eventual choice should not be properly described as 'free' because 'free' entails 'not caused' and all choices are in fact caused (though we may not be aware of this). We may not like the Hard Determinist's analysis of the concept of free choice, but there seems to be no 'denial of the obvious' as there is with the Eliminativist.

But does the Eliminativist really deny the obvious? It has recently become fashionable to emphasize the *theory-laden nature of all observation*. This emphasis is combined with the introduction of the notion of a folk theory, a pre-scientific sort of theory that is held in an unselfconscious, unarticulated manner by ordinary people, a theory that may go down to our simplest observations. Our belief that physical objects continue to exist when unobserved is a 'theory' of this sort. With these conceptions in place, it becomes possible to suggest that the existence of mentality and the mind is a bad theory that has crept into our ordinary thinking about the world.

The most ordinary observations, it is said, involve folk theory; some folk theory is bad; and all of it can be called upon to justify itself. This notion contrasts sharply with the older Cartesian epistemology that looks for indubitable foundations for knowledge and that, ironically, finds that foundation in the observation of our own mind.

I think that we want some intermediate position between the free-swinging epistemology of 'it's all theory' and the idea of an indubitable bedrock for knowledge. Perhaps we can find it in Wilfrid Sellars's important and helpful distinction between the *manifest* and the *scientific image* of the world. (See his classic paper "Philosophy and the Scientific Image of Man".) The manifest image is the image of the world obtained by ordinary observation: ordinary objects with familiar perceived properties standing in familiar perceived relations. In many ways it is quite a reliable image, though it is limited. It permits us to operate in the world with reasonable efficiency. Before the rise of organized inquiry, it was the only reasonably reliable image of the world that any human beings had. (Consider what cave-persons knew about the world.) Mental states and processes have their acknowledged place in the manifest image. The scientific image of the world goes far beyond the manifest image. It is the image that natural science, in particular physics and cosmology, is gradually building up for us. (The picture gets stranger every day!)

The manifest image is obviously seriously incomplete. And it involves a certain amount of error. A stock example is the relative emptiness of ordinary 'solid' objects. You can shoot 'fundamental particles' through them and hardly ever hit anything. But can the manifest image be as radically mistaken as Rorty, Feyerabend, and the Churchlands assume it is? In physical science we gradually advance to better and better theories, and so to a better 'scientific image'. But these theories have to pass the test of observation, and observation is soaked in the concepts and assumptions of the manifest image. The language of observation and testing generally is the language of the manifest image. Consider, for instance, how scientific observation involves reference to dials, pointer-readings, photographs, and computer screens. It also includes much mental language—perception, calculation, and thought, for instance. As a result, the manifest image is a branch that we cannot cut away entirely. A critique of the manifest image has to get its evidence from the manifest image. As a result, only if the image is *broadly* reliable can we cast doubt on some of its own features. ('Broadly' is a bit vague, but I do not see how to be more precise.) From this standpoint, cutting mentality out of the manifest image appears as an exceedingly radical move, and one that we should be rather sceptical about.

8.4. Eliminativism based on a semantic mistake?

It may be that Eliminativists are working, consciously or unconsciously, with a *descriptivist* theory of reference. For such a theory, to refer to something is to have one or more 'definite descriptions' or 'identifying descriptions' that pick it out as that thing. An Eliminativist such as Rorty then further assumes that, for mental phenomena, *being non-physical* is part of that description. (As perhaps it is for some people.) Eliminativists such as the Churchlands assume that the deliverances of neurophysiology show that the descriptions embedded in 'folk psychology' must be completely abandoned.

Nowadays, however, Causal theories of reference are more popular than Descriptivist ones. I have to be brief here, but the idea of a Causal theory of reference is that, at least for key objects and key types of objects, there should be a (suitable) causal chain stretching from the thing referred to, to the person who makes reference to that thing. Descriptions may come into reference, but a suitable causal chain from the thing referred to, to the person who makes the reference is also required. Once you have a theory of reference like this, the Eliminativist position looks less plausible.

Consider a certain brain process that an Eliminativist thinks is wrongly called pain. Presumably they would not deny that brain processes of this sort *cause* speakers to say things like "I'm in pain". This causal process may be of a highly particular sort. And, no doubt, if it is to count as *referring* to that brain process, it must also bring about certain classifyings, and certain describings, by the speaker. ("It is in my left hand; it is throbbing and unpleasant.") But will it be much different from the causal process that starts with, say, a cut in the finger and ends with the speaker saying "I've cut myself here"? The second remark definitely refers to a cut. Why doesn't the first remark refer to a pain? It is not plausible to say, "It isn't pain because pains are, for one reason or another, just a bad theory, and so the attempted reference did not succeed." We can ask the Eliminativist, "What was the person referring to, then?"

The only answer for the Eliminativist seems to be, "A brain process of a certain sort wrongly called pain." We can then ask the Eliminativist, "Why will not 'pain' do as its name then?" If the Eliminativist then says, "Because pains are just a bad theory. They do not exist" can we not reply, "OK. We did use to think that pains were non-physical, or we had other bad theories about them. Still, why not then keep the old name 'pain' and simply discard the old ideas about pain as dubious theories?"

The Eliminativist's position is not completely indefensible, but it does not seem at all plausible. It is not like the case of caloric fluid or witches where so much hangs on the question whether or not a certain description is true.

Notes

1. It should be noted that Rorty does not actually deny that sensations and other mental entities exist. Rather, he says that it is *plausible* to say, in the light of neurophysiological theory so far, that there are no mental entities. Feyerabend was less cautious.

Readings and references for Eliminativism

Churchland, P. M. 1984. *Matter and Consciousness*. Cambridge, Mass.: MIT Press, A Bradford Book.

Feyerabend, Paul. 1963. "Mental Events and the Brain." *The Journal of Philosophy* 60: pp. 295–296. Reprinted in Lycan, *Mind and Cognition.*

Lycan, William G. 1990. *Mind and Cognition.* Cambridge, Mass.: Blackwell.

Rorty, Richard. 1965. "Mind–Body Identity, Privacy, and Categories." *Review of Metaphysics* 19: pp. 25–54. Reprinted, together with other material on Eliminativism, in *Materialism and the Mind–Body Problem*, ed. David M. Rosenthal. New Jersey: Prentice-Hall, 1971.

_____. 1970. "Incorrigibility As a Mark of the Mental." *Journal of Philosophy* 67: pp. 399–424.

Rosenthal, David M. 1991. *The Nature of Mind.* New York: Oxford University Press.

Sellars, Wilfrid. 1963. "Philosophy and the Scientific Image of Man." Chap. 1 in *Science, Perception, and Reality.* London: Routledge and Kegan Paul.

CHAPTER NINE

Functionalism

A text for this section is Lycan, Mind and Cognition, *pp. 47–143.*

Functionalism is more or less the contemporary orthodoxy about the mind–body problem in analytic philosophy. We shall see that there are various varieties of Functionalism. (You can say that the Causal theory is one of these varieties: Causal Functionalism.)

9.1. Token–token versus type–type identity

Jerry Fodor, who is or was perhaps the leading Functionalist, published back in 1968 (in *Psychological Explanation*) an attack on Place's model for mental/physical identity: "lightning is an electric discharge". He said that the lightning case was a case of *micro-reduction* similar to "a table is a collection of molecules" or "heat is motion of constituent molecules". The proper model, he said, is an assertion that something identified in terms of *function* (the mental side) is the very same thing as something identified in terms of nature (brain processes).

The notion of 'function' is not entirely clear. Is it what a thing does, or what it is supposed to do? Lewis's notion of causal role is at least close to what Fodor was thinking about. And if you take function as causal role, you can see that the left-hand (mental) side of Place's formula will not fit causal role. The concept of lightning is just the notion of a certain sort of observable happening, a sort of flash, in the sky. It is not a causal concept. There seems to be nothing wrong with the right-hand (physical) side. The *natures* that Fodor mentions are brain processes. So, surely, despite what Fodor himself said, we do have a micro-reductive identification on the right-hand side. It is the left-hand side of the Place model, the lightning side, that is wrong because it is not a matter of causal role.

At this point, it seems that Brian Medlin's "the gene is the DNA molecule" would give Fodor what he wants. 'Gene' is certainly a causal, or functional, concept; 'DNA molecule' gives the micro-reductive physical nature. I don't know if Fodor had even heard of Medlin's analogy at the time that he rejected Place's model, but even if he had, he might well have rejected it. The reason for this is that Medlin's example is rather naturally taken as an example of a *type–type* identity, but Fodor thinks that in the mind/brain case there is only *token–token identity*.

The useful distinction between type and token was introduced by C. S. Peirce, the great nineteenth-century U.S. philosopher. It is pretty much the traditional distinction between universal and particular. Consider the simple display in Figure 9.1. How many words does this display contain? Only one type: the word 'the'. But it contains two *tokens* of this type. The distinction just applied to words can be applied quite generally: to swans, floods, electrons, sensations, brain processes. It is topic neutral.

"Lightning is an electric discharge", "the gene is the DNA molecule", and "pain is the firing of x-fibres" are all type–type identities. Being of the type lightning is being of the type electric discharge, and so for the other two identities. Type–type identities entail the corresponding token–token identities. If pain is the firing of x-fibres, then each token of pain is a token of a firing of x-fibres.

Suppose, however, that one particular token is a firing of x-fibres. Does this token–token identity ensure the corresponding type-identity? Fodor pointed out that it does not. After all, is it not possible for different mechanisms to perform the same function (to play the same causal role)? Consider recording the time. It can be done by sun dial, water clock, a mechanism using a spring to drive pointers on a dial, or electronically. All these different sorts of things do the same thing: tell the time. Consider also computers. Computational states are characterized *functionally*, as steps in the realization of a certain programme, a programme given by the software that the computer is using. But the same steps can be *realized* by all sorts of different mechanisms, all sorts of different hardware. (A point strongly urged by Hilary Putnam.)

FIGURE 9.1   Types and Tokens

THE	THE

The upshot, according to Fodor, is that you can't make identifications of the form *pain is firing of x-fibres*. The relation between mental type and physical type is not necessarily one–one (it is likely, one–many), yet a one–one relation is needed if we are to advance the claim of *identity*. It may be that in human beings pain is always firing of x-fibres. But what of the other animals? It would be *species chauvinism* to assume that all pain was firing of x-fibres. And if an electronic mind could ever be constructed, a possibility that cannot be ruled out (although no present computer or other device has a mind, or comes close to having one), there might be pain without any brain process at all. The Identity theory, Fodor argued, had overlooked this point, as shown by their suggested models. The best you can realistically hope for is token–token identity.

We can now see why Fodor would probably have considered "the gene is the DNA molecule" to be an unsatisfactory model for mental/physical identity. The model suggests type–type identity. So Fodor wants a different model. The one he comes up with instead is "Valve-lifters (some of them) are camshafts". The concept of a valve-lifter is clearly a functional concept. There is function on the left-hand side. On the right-hand side: A camshaft is a shaft having a special shape, so that, as the shaft rotates, it lifts open the valve and then lets it fall. But the type valve-lifter cannot be identified with the type camshaft because valves in engines can be lifted by other means, for instance by push-rods. We can say only that *this* valve-lifter is a camshaft. (Actually, as Sterelny points out, different DNA sequences can sometimes function as the same gene, that is, play the same causal role in the genetic process. So it seems that Medlin's model can even accommodate Fodor's point.)

Indeed, token–token identity is too cautious a reaction to the type–type identities envisaged by Identity theorists. It is natural to think that in, say, the same species, or some subtype of the same species, it is the same *sort* of brain process or state that plays the *same* functional role. This gives you a more restricted type–type identity. Fodor had quite an important point to make, but he may have pushed it a bit too hard.

9.1.1. A consequence for psychology

As a result of his criticism of type–type identity, Fodor denied that there could be any reduction of psychological to physiological types. *Laws*, laws of nature, however, link types with types. So Fodor denied that there could be any reduction of psychological laws to physiological laws. He was here rejecting the view put forward by Paul Oppenheim and Hilary Putnam in a 1958 paper titled "The Unity of Science as a Working Hypothesis". They had reasoned that a psychological law correlates psychological types with psychological types, that the psychological types could be identified with physiological types, thus reducing the psychological law to a physiological law. Physiological types could in turn be identified with physico-chemical types; chemistry is reducible to physics, and so in the end psychological laws would turn out to be (highly particular) physical laws.

But all this depends upon type–type identities being established, and, for the reason given, Fodor thought there was little prospect of that. Psychological laws, and, for that same reason, physiological laws, would have to remain unreduced. (See the introduction to Fodor's book, *The Language of Thought*).

9.1.2. But the thesis of Physicalism seems unaffected

Fodor's point, of real importance, nevertheless led to confusion about Physicalism. He thought that a Physicalist (a Materialist) is committed to the thesis of the unity of science. He therefore thought that he had given reasons to reject Physicalism.

In fact, however, the central core of Physicalism, the metaphysical core, remains unaffected. Fodor's argument is perfectly compatible with the proposition that each mental token (each having of a pain, etc.) is a purely physical affair. Grant, for the sake of argument, that there is no physiological pain-type but instead only an indefinitely large disjunction of physiological types. All the same, each token of having a pain can still be a purely physical state of the brain. Nothing but a physical thing and physical properties need be involved.

Consider Fodor's valve-lifters. Whether they are camshafts or push rods, they are pieces of machinery. What Michael Devitt calls 'the Physicalist dream'—the Physicalist ontology—remains unaffected by Fodor's point. It is true, though, that this ontological point can, in considerable degree, be neglected in psychology. Contemporary psychologists, even where they are quite happy to identify mental processes with neural processes, do not have much need to descend to physiological detail. They think of the central nervous system as an *information processing system*, the most sophisticated information processing system to be found in the body. It extracts information from the environment via the senses and processes it (for the most part at a totally unconscious level), thus enabling the organism to react back on its environment where this is appropriate. It does not really matter just how the brain carries out these information processing procedures.

9.2. Varieties of Functionalism

Some of the main varieties of Functionalism are Machine Functionalism, Homuncular Functionalism, and Teleological Functionalism. And as mentioned previously, the Causal theory can be thought of as a variety of Functionalism. I will not say much more about the original Machine Functionalism, a position pioneered by Hilary Putnam. It has not lived on because of the rather narrow conception of a machine that it worked with. (But for a careful and useful discussion, see Jaegwon Kim's *Philosophy of Mind*, chap. 4, and the quite long index entry under "Functionalism: Machine" in Lycan's *Mind and Cognition*.) The general idea is to compare the mind to a computer, with mental states as the computational states of the computer and these states characterized in terms of the programme, the software. One thing about this idea is perfectly clear: The 'programme' running in our brain will have to be unlike any programme that can be written at present, and in the foreseeable future.

At the same time, though, the general inspiration of Machine Functionalism has lived on. The idea that the brain, and therefore the mind, operates in a way at least comparable to a computer, together with the closely connected notion that the brain/mind is an information-processing mechanism, have had a deep influence on contemporary philosophy and psychology.

9.2.1. Homuncular Functionalism

In giving psychological explanations, it is extremely easy to think in terms of *homunculi*, of little persons. The mind is obviously an extremely complex, complexly interrelated, object. How are we to analyze what goes on in perception, in purposive action, in deliberation followed by decision, and so on? It is tempting to use the model of a society or a team of little persons who cooperate to bring about a certain result. For instance, there will be little persons who store information in memory banks, others who retrieve it, others who ponder what to do with the retrieved information—the last lot perhaps will be a whole committee of ponderers, having different interests and purposes.

There is a standard reply to suggestions of this sort: They are useless and misleading because they involve a vicious regress. How is seeing done? It is a tempting picture that there is a little person who looks out from the eyes. There is the poetic, and attractive, conceit that the eyes are the window of the soul. But won't the little person need to have eyes? And these eyes will need a still littler person to look out of the little eyes, ad infinitum.

Remember how Ryle argues against *acts* of will (things the person does, and can be held responsible for) as causes of our actions. If such an act is needed as a cause, he says, then it will have to be caused by a further act of will, and so on forever. This was one horn of Ryle's dilemma for the causal theory of the will. The argument against the little persons is essentially the same argument, and it looks to be a strong one. A 'little person' picture *anthropormorphizes* the inner causes, the inner carriers out of mental functions. Persons are explained in terms of persons!

Yet the homuncular fantasy does seem a helpful analogy in characterizing the operations of the mind. Can we rescue it? Dan Dennett has done so. (See, for instance, his "Why the Law of Effect Will Not Go Away", p. 70 especially.) What we must do, he says, is go with the regress. Allow little persons within the real person, still littler persons within those persons, and so on as far as needed. But at each step the persons must be *stupider* and must be more and more narrowly focussed in their function. They do less and less, and they do it (or fail to do it, sometimes) in a more and more automatic and routine fashion. Eventually, you get back to little persons who are so stupid and who perform such a low-grade action that all they do, for instance, is carry a simple message from A to B in the brain. And at that point, says Dennett, you 'discharge' your little persons, substituting instead, say, a neuron firing and sending an impulse to another neuron. With the bottom level 'physicalized', you can go back up the layers of little persons, discharging them at each point. (It sounds a bit like unemployment caused by technological advances!)

So, *in the end*, the Homuncular Functionalist sees intelligent processing of information and intelligent behaviour as caused by a huge mass of unintelligent processes. But the unintelligent processes are complexly and *hierarchically* organized, and this organization gives us the intelligent mind. Each step up the hierarchy sophisticates the process a bit more. Of course, most of this is programme, not performance, but it looks to be the way that a Materialist ought to go.

Suppose that you were a tiny creature who could travel inside the brain at the neuronal level. It seems clear that you would never see thoughts or anything else mental. But is this an argument against Materialism? Leibniz seems to have thought it was. (See his *Monadology*, sec. 17.) The Materialist can reply by saying that in this situation you would be seeing the trees and not the wood. But, the Materialist can add, if you could see the wood, grasping all its incredible hierarchical and functional complexity, and also grasping what it is capable of giving rise to in the way of behaviour, then you would be seeing the mentality of the brain processes.

9.2.2. Teleological Functionalism

Consider a sensation of something green. It is characteristically caused by green objects acting on our eyes. It also enables us, if we so purpose, to select the green object from other things in our environment. These are *causal* platitudes and are the sort of thing that a Causal Functionalist relies upon. But can we not say something more? Can we not say that this is what sensations of something green are *for*? They exist in order for us to react selectively to green things—to leaves, grass, unripe fruit, and so on—in our environment. Mental entities seem to have functions in this *teleological* sense.

Could the *telos* or end of mental states and processes be objective features of them, and not simply a way that we happen to regard and value them? If so, then these objective features would be an important part of mental states and processes, perhaps part of our concept of them, or at least of our 'identifying descriptions' of them (Michael Levin), if you do not much like the idea of conceptual analysis.

But how can the Materialist embrace *objective* teleology? Was not the path to an objective science opened up by Descartes when he threw out the old Aristotelian final causes and looked for efficient causes only in the bodily realm? Humans and animals have purposes, but the heart has no purpose, and neither has a sensation of something green.

For the case of certain concepts, however, a rather ironic dialectic operates. At a certain point in the advance of a subject, a particular notion may be a hindrance to the development of that subject. It becomes necessary to thrust it aside in order to break up the thought patterns associated with that concept and to direct research energy elsewhere. But after the subject has developed further, it may become evident that the old, discredited notion did have some positive value. It may then be possible to re-introduce the notion in a suitably purged and chastened form. I think that this has happened to teleology.

The Mechanist-Physicalist view that biologists adopted with the rise of scientific biology and physiology made them think that what a thing is *for* is a disreputable notion. And yet: Is not the eye for seeing, and the heart for pumping the blood? If you are trying to understand a biological mechanism, it often provides a valuable clue to its operation to consider its function, in the sense of what it is for. Despite their official ideology, biologists do this all the time. So the question arises: While holding fast to a Physicalist world view, or at least to a Physicalist account of the operation of organisms, is it possible to find a Physicalist-respectable account of function and teleology?

A certain amount of work has been done on this problem recently. The obvious place to start is from the fact that organisms are evolved beings, and from the 'mechanism' by which it is generally accepted that this evolution occurred: the mechanism of natural selection. The eye is for seeing. What can we mean by this, thinking naturalistically, physicalistically? Well, the eye was actually caused to come into existence (more precisely, mechanisms that were more and more light-sensitive were caused to come into existence) as a *causal result* of the fact that proto-eyes and then eyes were advantageous things to have. This advantage was objective because organisms having these organs tended to do better relative to organisms of the same type but lacking these organs. Since the improvements were genetically caused, they could be passed on to descendants, descendants who would have an evolutionary advantage over the organisms that lacked the improvements. So we can see, without going into details, that for an organ to have a certain function is for it to have certain powers, powers that were caused to come into existence as a result of the fact that developing such powers conferred evolutionary advantage. (See Lycan, *Mind and Cognition*, pt. II, sec. 4–6.)

If something along these lines is correct, then one can apply it to many mental entities, taken as types. One can say that selecting green objects out from other objects is the teleological function of the having of sensations of green things. That is what green sensations are for. That is why we have these colour-sensations.

The philosopher who, more than anyone, has argued for a teleological view of the mind is Ruth Millikan. Her book *Language, Thought, and Other Biological Categories* (1984) has been a major influence. It is, unfortunately for students, a particularly difficult work. However, a collection of her papers devoted to this topic, *White Queen Psychology* (1993), is more accessible.

It can be seen that Homuncular and Teleological Functionalisms go together naturally, and perhaps blend with each other at the edges. Furthermore, a Causal-Homuncular-Teleological synthesis of some sort would seem to be a natural way to develop Functionalism.

Readings and references for Functionalism

Dennett, Daniel C. 1990. "Why the Law of Effect Will Not Go Away." In *Mind and Cognition*, ed. William G. Lycan, pp. 63–77. Cambridge, Mass.: Blackwell.

Fodor, Jerry A. 1968. *Psychological Explanation*. New York: Random House.

_____. 1975. *The Language of Thought*. New York: Thomas Y. Crowell.

Kim, Jaegwon. 1996. *Philosophy of Mind*. Boulder, Colo.: Westview Press.

Leibniz, G. W. 1714. *The Monadology*. In *Leibniz: Philosophical Writings*, ed. and trans. Mary Morris. London: J. M. Dent & Sons, Everyman, 1934.

Lycan, William G. 1990. *Mind and Cognition*, Cambridge, Mass.: Blackwell.

Millikan, Ruth. 1984. *The Language of Thought and Other Biological Categories*. Cambridge, Mass.: MIT Press, A Bradford Book.

———. 1990. *White Queen Psychology*. Cambridge, Mass.: MIT Press, A Bradford Book.

Oppenheim, Paul, and Hilary Putnam. 1958. "Unity of Science As a Working Hypothesis." In *Minnesota Studies in the Philosophy of Science*. Vol.11, ed. Herbert Feigl, Michael Scriven, and Grover Maxwell, pp. 3–36. Minneapolis: University of Minnesota Press.

CHAPTER TEN

Consciousness

A text for this chapter is section X of The Nature of Consciousness, *edited by Ned Block, Owen Flanagan, and Güven Güzeldere.*

We will finish this book by looking at what I regard as the most serious problems for a Materialist account of the mind. If the Materialist can get over these difficulties, then I think that other difficulties that can be raised are much less serious. I am going to argue that these 'serious problems' can be solved. You will, of course, be aware that there are plenty of good analytic philosophers who think that one or more of these problems cannot be solved: that Materialism is false. And even among the Materialists there will be plenty of philosophers who think that one or more of my suggested solutions are quite wrong, and even that I have neglected the *real* problems. You have been warned!

As I see it, the central difficulties are:

1. consciousness
2. qualia (the sensible qualities)
3. intentionality (the 'aboutness' of the mental)

We begin with consciousness.

What we have here is really a *challenge*. Many people just cannot see how a purely material system can possibly be conscious. Materialists, such as myself, need to answer this challenge by producing a plausible theory of what consciousness is. As a matter of fact, the account of consciousness to be developed in this chapter will not answer the challenge fully. This is because the account will use the

111

notion of *representation*, and an anti-Materialist may fairly ask how a purely material thing can ever really represent anything. An account of representation itself that is compatible with Materialism will have to wait until we reach the problem of intentionality in Chapter 12.

But now for the account of consciousness. We begin by doing some sorting out. It seems that there is not just one notion of consciousness but a number of related notions that easily get confused with each other. I am going to distinguish between:

1. minimal consciousness
2. perceptual consciousness
3. introspective consciousness

The first two can be dealt with fairly briskly. It is introspective consciousness that demands the most attention.

10.1. Minimal consciousness

Minimal consciousness, as I define it, is no more than this: the occurrence in the mind of some mental event or process. The contrast here is with what we can call 'the completely stopped mind', a notion we have already met with in criticizing Descartes' idea that the mind is, of necessity, always active. The completely stopped mind is a mind in which there is nothing mental *happening*. A stopped mind would still have a great deal in it. There would be knowledge and beliefs of all sorts. There would be memories. There would be all sorts of skills and know how. There would be all sorts of long-term purposes, and all sorts of attitudes to the world. But these things would be like unmanifested dispositions. They wouldn't be going anywhere. A good model is a fully programmed computer that is switched off. The program is there and ready to go, but it isn't going anywhere computationally.

Unlike the computer, however, there is some reason to believe that the totally stopped mind is no more than an idealization, something never fully reached. Perhaps it can be approached in dreamless sleep, and still more nearly in deep unconsciousness without brain death. But anaesthetized patients, for instance, can react in a small degree to somebody saying their name in their ear, suggesting that their mind is functioning in some minimal way. In any case, the idealization is useful, enabling us to see, by means of a contrast, what minimal consciousness involves. Dreaming is minimal consciousness, and so is the slow thinking that is now thought to occur even in the periods of dreamless sleep, for these are forms of mental activity.

As just mentioned, the notion of the stopped mind is an anti-Cartesian notion, not in the sense of an anti-Dualist notion—a Cartesian Dualist can make sense of the notion of the stopped mind—but in the sense of rejecting Descartes' doctrine that consciousness is the *essence* of the mental. The mind can exist in the absence of even minimal consciousness.

10.2. Perceptual consciousness

To have perceptual consciousness you have to be perceiving the world. When one is awake one has perceptual consciousness. Being awake as human beings are awake, however, is not the case that we should concentrate on. The reason for this is that at least for most of the time that adult human beings are awake, they are also in some degree introspectively conscious. This fact leads to the muddling of the two notions of perceptual consciousness and introspective consciousness, and we need to separate them. It is better, I think, to go way down the evolutionary ladder to quite primitive animals. Let us consider a lizard.

Suppose a lizard is awake. The lizard has eyes and other sense organs, including organs that give it information about its own body. So surely, then, it perceives. But if it perceives, then it has a mental life, even if at a primitive level. It seems unlikely, though, that it has any introspective consciousness. Suppose that it does not. Then it has perceptual consciousness without introspective consciousness. That is the sort of case that we want for bringing out the nature of perceptual consciousness and distinguishing it from introspective consciousness.

Consider a lizard that is awake and seeing the world from its rather limited perspective (a perspective that at present we know little about!). Now suppose that we put a bowl over the lizard so that suddenly it is not able to see anything except the darkness. Presumably it can register the darkness and react to it in some way. (Perhaps by doing nothing.) But can it be aware that its seeing has stopped? I would suppose that it cannot. For to be aware that seeing had stopped, as opposed to merely registering the darkness, would be for the lizard to be aware of a change in its own mental processes. And that would take it from perceptual to *introspective* consciousness.

That is why a human being awake is not a good case to focus upon if we want to grasp the notion of perceptual consciousness. For in the normal waking state, we are not merely perceptually conscious of the world; we are also aware (conscious) that we are perceiving the world. The lizard, while awake, has representations of the current state of the world, representations of the current state of its own body, and of some of the relations that its body has to the world. (Some of these representations may be incorrect. Why should lizards be free from sensory illusion?) We also perceive. But *in addition*, we represent to ourselves our own current mental states, including a representing of our own perceptual representations. And this higher-order representation goes beyond mere perceptual consciousness. What we have in representing a perceptual representation is introspective consciousness.

10.3. Introspective consciousness

I am assuming here the traditional doctrine of introspection: that each of us has the power to become directly aware of some of the things that currently go on in our own mind, and in a 'direct' way, unlike the more indirect awareness we have of what goes on in the minds of others. I am rejecting the Cartesian-inspired view that this awareness is infallible, and I reject even more strongly the view, also Cartesian-inspired, that this awareness extends to the *whole* of what is currently going on in our mind. No human faculty is infallible, no human faculty is all-embracing. But introspection exists all right. John Locke called it 'reflection' and likened it to an inner sense. Kant took up Locke's idea and actually called it 'inner sense'. It seems to be not unlike sense perception. For instance, it would seem that you don't need language for it.

Introspection can be something we deliberately *do;* it can be an *act* of ours: turning our gaze into our own breast as Hume puts it. It is then like, say, looking deliberately around a room. But deliberately introspecting is rather a sophisticated thing to do. We may contrast it with mere *introspective awareness*, where we simply become aware of some current mental content, in the same sort of way that, in vision, we become aware that something or other is before us. Introspective awareness can be of a very 'reflex' sort. The introspecting mechanism, whatever it is, does no more than keep a watching brief on our own current mental contents, but without making much of a deal about it. The 'whatever it is' serves to remind us that we have, at present, little scientific knowledge of this faculty, and we may expect some surprises in the future, as study of the brain, and with it the psychology of introspective consciousness, advances. But I do not believe that the simple things I have said so far will be found to be seriously incorrect.

Can human beings have perceptual consciousness without introspective consciousness? The answer is surely, "Yes". In the field of perception, *subliminal* perception seems to be a reality. (See, for instance, N. F. Dixon, *Subliminal Perception*.) Thoughts and conduct can be affected by the action of objects on our sense organs in such a manner as to suggest that perception was present, although we were not aware that it was present. My favourite case is that of the long-distance truck driver who, after driving for many hours, may 'blank out' and then come to, many miles later. You have perhaps experienced this yourself. It is an alarming experience. There must have been perception during that period, or else the truck would have quickly been off the road. My interpretation of such events is that introspective consciousness is switched off, but perceptual consciousness remains. The introspective unconsciousness of the driver is not, as it were, particularly deep. It can 'switch on' again fairly easily. That is not the case in all cases of subliminal perception. But I think that these are only differences of degree.

Kim Sterelny suggests to me that what may be happening in the long-distance truck driver case is that introspective awareness actually continues, but it fails in this special sort of case to lay down any memory traces. This is certainly a possibility, and in the present state of our knowledge it cannot be ruled out. But it remains a useful case for us here because it at least *seems* to be a case of perceptual consciousness without introspective consciousness.

Subliminal perception is *unconscious* perception, and there is much evidence that other sorts of mental events and processes may occur, or mental states may obtain, in the absence of consciousness. Whatever we think of Freudian psychology, it seems clear that we can have thoughts, desires, wishes that we are not aware of having, perhaps as a result of 'repressing' them from consciousness because we do not wish to acknowledge them. But there are all sorts of unconscious mental processing that we do—for instance the process of constructing more or less grammatical sentences—that are not at all the result of repression. Constructing sentences involves complex grammatical operations that must surely be classified as mental, but they are not accessible to consciousness. 'Unconscious' here, I think, must mean 'not the object of introspective awareness', and 'not accessible to consciousness' must mean 'not capable of being accessed by introspection'.

Introspective awareness presumably comes relatively late in the evolutionary development. The lizard does not have it. We would expect that only with the mammals, and perhaps only with the higher mammals, does introspective awareness emerge.

Like perception, introspection is a matter of representation. But it is representation with a narrow domain: nothing but the representer's own (current) mental life. It can seem rather a mystifying thing, and it would help if we could find a demystifying model for it. It would also help if we could discover its evolutionary purpose, could discover what introspection is *for*. Let us address these two concerns.

First a model. Besides the traditional 'five senses'—sight, hearing, taste, smell, touch—there is also bodily perception. This is our awareness of current goings on in, and current states of, our own body, where this awareness is *not* derived from the five senses. Bodily perception breaks down into a number of systems. Kinaesthetic sensations advise us of the motion and position of our limbs; our sense of balance tells us how we are oriented to the earth; sensations of heat and cold tell us of the temperature of the body and its parts; pains, itches, tickles, and so on tell us of major and minor unpleasantnesses at places in the body. Without these systems we would be in a bad way.

Bodily perception is, for each of us, confined to our own body. Each of us has a series of systems that monitors our own body. These systems are not infallible, of course, and they are certainly not all-embracing, but they are of the utmost importance in our life. Particularly important, and central to our awareness of ourselves as individuals, is what is called the *proprioceptive* system, which Oliver Sacks describes as:

that continuous but unconscious sensory flow from the moveable parts of our body (muscles, tendons, joints), by which their position and tone and motion is continually monitored and adjusted, but in a way which is hidden from us because it is automatic and unconscious. (1986, p. 42.)

This quotation comes from Sacks's essay "The Disembodied Lady", which appears in his book *The Man Who Mistook His Wife for a Hat.* The essay describes the utterly disorienting and horrible things that happen to a person when their proprioceptive system ceases functioning.

The importance of proprioception and the other modes of bodily perception for us here is that they give us an unmysterious model for introspection. Introspection is a system, one that we still hardly understand in physiological terms, by which we monitor our own mind. In bodily perception, the mind monitors its own body. In introspection, the mind monitors itself.

We can easily see the point of bodily perception and why it should evolve. Speaking teleologically, we can see what it is *for.* But why do we have introspection? What is *it* for? One theory is that it has a great *social* importance. We are profoundly social beings and our interactions with our conspecifics (other human beings!) are therefore peculiarly important biologically. If we can know something about our own mind—if we are self-conscious in this sense—then, assuming other people's minds work much the same as ours, we will have a source of information as to what other people's motives, beliefs, and so on are or might be. So we will be better equipped to interact with them.

This is a valuable suggestion, I think. But the importance of access to our own minds goes well beyond this. In the animal kingdom, a particular evolutionary strategy has been followed, at least by human beings, and perhaps by some of the higher mammals, especially the apes. It is the policy of thinking, planning, before one acts. We have followed it with truly remarkable results. (For me, a paradigm is provided by the psychologist Wolfgang Kohler's ape. A banana was hung from the ceiling, higher than the ape could reach. But two boxes lay in the room. After a period of frustration, and apparent thought, the ape rushed to the boxes, dragged them under

the banana, and put them one on top of the other. In a moment he
had the banana.)

Now, thinking as a means to acting is itself a species of action,
purposive action. It is not like ideas just passing through the mind,
as in the association of ideas. It is doing something purposive inside
the head, usually as a means to doing something outside the head.
We have already had occasion to talk about purposes in the discussion of the Causal theory. Purposes are information-driven causes
driving (not always successfully) towards the thing purposed. The
information that feeds into the purpose that is driving the organism
is knowledge, belief, know how, and *perception*. Perception is absolutely vital for action in the physical sphere. Only perception provides the *feedback* that must exist in order for the purposer to adjust
behaviour according to the circumstances as they develop along the
path to the goal, and, finally, in order for the purposer to perceive
that the end has been achieved. You cannot do the simplest thing in
the world, even put up your arm, much less cross the room, without
elaborate perceptual feedback.

What then of action inside the mind? How is the mind to get the
needed feedback on its operations and recognize that these operations have reached a certain terminus, unless it, also, can know how
the mental scene develops? Ordinary perception, even bodily perception, is no use here, because it is not directed within the mind.
Had there not better be a substitute? The substitute, I suggest, is
provided by 'inner' perception, inner sense, introspective consciousness. That, I hypothesize, is what introspective awareness is
for. That is why it evolved.

As already mentioned, during ordinary waking life for human beings we are not only aware of perception and various other mental
processes going on the whole time, but we are fairly continuously
introspectively aware that these things are going on in our mind.
Particularly, we not only perceive, but we are aware of our perceiving. The introspection may be unselfconscious and low key, but it is
generally there. Why is this so? I suggest that introspection exists
because 'inner sense' has a 'watching brief' (as the lawyers say). At
any time, something that demands *thought* and attention may tran-
spire in our body and environment. Continuous but 'reflex' introspective attention to our perceptions, in particular, is an alarm system that keeps us ready to bring thought and attention to bear if it is

needed. And, as already suggested in the previous paragraph, once thought and attention are in play, introspective awareness will be needed for the carrying out of any purposive *mental* activity that seems necessary.

So I think a reasonably plausible explanation can be given both of why introspective awareness exists at all, and also of why it is so continuously present in the waking life of human beings. Introspection is itself a mental happening, or in some cases a deliberate mental action. Since it is something that goes on in the mind, we would expect that we could have introspective awareness of introspection. Indeed, that seems to be the case. If one is asked to introspect, one is likely to be aware, introspectively aware it would seem, that one is introspecting. But this might seem to lead to a vicious regress. If I can be introspectively aware that I am introspecting, can I not be introspectively aware that all this is going on, and so on, ad infinitum?

I don't think that this regress follows at all. All that follows is that *at some point* the chain of introspections of introspections of . . . must come to a halt. There must be an introspective awareness that is itself not the subject of introspection: an unscanned scanner so to speak. At what point the regress ends is an empirical question, not to be settled *a priori*. What the physical mechanism of all this is, we have at present little idea.

Perceiving is first-order representation, a representation of the world around us, our own body, and the relations in which our body stands to that world. It is, of course, a highly selective representation, and it can be erroneous. When we are *aware* of having perceptions we are having second-order awarenesses: awarenesses of awareness, representations of representations. The second-order awareness is *also* selective, and there can be, for instance, perceptions that we are not aware of having (subliminal perceptions).

Consciousness, then, both perceptual consciousness and introspective consciousness, is representation. An anti-Materialist might still object that it is not clear how a purely material system could represent, and that it is particularly unclear that a purely material system is capable of the sophisticated representations, including the representations of representations, that we are capable of. The point is well taken. But the difficulty about representation is the difficulty of intentionality, the third of our three problems, and the subject of Chapter 12. Representations are about, or point to, the things they represent, things that may not even exist. How can a purely material system do this? We will leave the problem for now and go on to consider the difficulty about the sensible qualities, more generally, the problem about qualia.

Readings and references for consciousness

Just recently, there has been quite a lot of interesting work on consciousness, although the notion has not always been well sorted out from the notions of qualia and intentionality.

Block, Ned, Owen Flanagan, and Güven Güzeldere, eds. 1997. *The Nature of Consciousness*. Cambridge, Mass.: MIT Press, A Bradford Book. See in particular part X: "Higher-Order Monitoring Conceptions of Consciousness.

Cassam, Quassim, ed. 1994. *Self-Knowledge*. Oxford Readings in Philosophy. Oxford: Oxford University Press.

Dennett, Daniel C. 1991. *Consciousness Explained*. Boston: Little, Brown, and Co.

Dixon, N. F. 1971. *Subliminal Perception: The Nature of a Controversy*. London: McGraw-Hill.

Dretske, Fred. 1993. "Conscious Experience." *Mind* 102: pp. 263–283.

Flanagan, Owen. *Consciousness Reconsidered*. Cambridge, Mass.: MIT Press, A Bradford Book.

Lycan, William G. 1996. *Consciousness and Experience*. Cambridge, Mass.: MIT Press, A Bradford Book.

Lyons, William. 1986. *The Disappearance of Introspection*. Cambridge, Mass.: MIT Press, A Bradford Book.

Sacks, Oliver. 1986. *The Man Who Mistook His Wife for a Hat*. London: Picador Books.

CHAPTER ELEVEN

The Sensible Qualities

A text for this chapter is William G. Lycan, Mind and Cognition, *section 7.*

11.1. The Qualia problem—how it arose

We may begin the discussion of 'the Qualia problem'—which seems to arouse more passion than anything else in the philosophy of mind!—by considering a closely connected problem, the problem of the *secondary qualities*. We saw this latter problem come up at the very beginning of the revival of Materialism about the mind in contemporary philosophy. In his paper "Sensations and Brain Processes" Smart tried to attack the problem in the course of a discussion of colour. The view he took then was too behaviouristic, but I think he was right to see how important the problem was. In my view it is the key to unlocking the problem about qualia, though relatively few philosophers have perceived that this is so. I must warn right away that the discussion in this chapter is likely to be found more difficult (and controversial) than anything else in this book.

The trouble with the secondary qualities begins back in the beginning of the seventeenth century, with the rise of modern science. Here is Galileo in 1623:

> I feel myself impelled by the necessity, as soon as I conceive a piece of matter or corporeal substance, of conceiving that in its own nature it is bounded and figured in such and such a figure, that in relation to others it is large or small, that it is in this or that place, in this or that time, that it is in motion or remains at rest, that it touches or does not touch another body, that it is single, few, or many; in short by no imagina-

tion can a body be separated from such conditions; but that it must be white or red, bitter or sweet, sounding or mute, of a pleasant or unpleasant odour, I do not perceive my mind forced to acknowledge it necessarily accompanied by such conditions; so if the senses were not the escorts, perhaps the reason or the imagination by itself would never have arrived at them. Hence I think that these tastes, odours, colours, etc., on the side of the object in which they seem to exist, are nothing else than mere names, but hold their residence in the sensitive body; so that if the animal were removed, every such quality would be abolished and annihilated. (*Il Saggiotore*, quoted by E. A. Burtt, *The Metaphysical Foundations of Modern Physical Science*, p. 89)

Variations on this theme have been found ever since. This, or something like this, has become the conventional opinion, spreading widely into all educated thought. The advantage of this view for a physicist, as Galileo was, is that colours, sounds, tastes, and smells do not have to be considered by physics. The physicist is free to concentrate upon such properties as mass, shape and size, velocity, acceleration, and so on, which turn out to be the important properties of matter if you are trying to find out the laws of its behaviour. The colours, sounds, smells and such can be swept away into the mind. They were later christened the secondary qualities by Robert Boyle, a phrase that was taken up into philosophy by John Locke.

Galileo does not mention them, but there is another group of qualities that appear to be in the mind in any case. Consider the sensations of ache, pain, itch, and tickle. Since these are sensations, they are in the mind. Does not each sort have its own special feel? They seem each to have qualities associated with them. Indeed, it seems to be these special qualities that make them the sensations that they are. So why not locate the secondary qualities in the mind along with these bodily sensations and their qualities, which, it seems, have to be in the mind anyway?

But, as we have already noted in 6.4, when discussing the Identity theory of the mind, if we want to be Materialists about the mind, this doctrine of the secondary qualities returns to haunt us. If the mind, or perceptions in particular, have these qualities, then the mind becomes something that has properties that nothing else physical has. How are we going to physicalize these qualities? It is not at all clear. Part of the trouble is their relative simplicity and their apparent unanalyzability. One point that it seems particularly important to stress is that no *functional* account of their nature (causal, homuncular, or teleological) seems to have much plausibility.

A further problem is that if the secondary qualities are 'pushed into the mind' they threaten to drag with them all other sensible qualities, for instance perceived shapes and motions. Berkeley, back in the eighteenth century, put the problem neatly:

> If you will trust your senses, is it not plain all sensible qualities coexist, or to them [the senses] appear as being in the same place? Do they ever represent a motion, or figure, as being divested of all other visible and tangible qualities? (First Dialogue, in *Berkeley's Philosophical Writings*, pp. 157–158)

If the 'secondary qualities' are to go into the mind, must not *all* the sensible qualities go into the mind? At that point, and remembering the bodily sensations, the problem of the secondary qualities has widened to become 'the Qualia problem'.

The Qualia problem haunts contemporary philosophy of mind. 'Qualia freaks' (to use the elegant name often given to upholders of the view that perception, and so the mind, does involve these inner qualities) mostly think that the qualia constitute a major objection to Materialist views of the mind. It is true that some Materialists think that we can accept the Galilean idea but go on to physicalize the sensations of secondary qualities, that is, to identify them with purely material processes in the brain. Nobody seems to have worked this idea out at all thoroughly, but it will probably have to be combined with what is called an 'error theory' of the secondary qualities. On that sort of theory it is allowed that we do *seem* to locate these qualities in the physical world. That seems completely right as a point of phenomenology. Colours, for instance, seem to be 'painted onto' surfaces of objects. But then the error theory suggests that there are in fact no such properties in the physical world. There are only the mistaken perceptions in the mind. These in turn will then have to be physicalized. This is Eliminativism about the secondary qualities. I think that this is a rather desperate view, which will involve many of the same difficulties as Eliminativism about the mental generally. We should adopt such a view only as a last resort.

11.2. An objectivist account of the secondary qualities

For myself, I think that the only plausible way that a Materialist can deal with the secondary qualities is completely to reverse the whole programme started by Galileo, a programme that has persisted for so long. What we should do is *put these qualities back into the physical world again.*

But we cannot put them back into the world *alongside* and in *addition* to the properties that contemporary science attributes to physical objects. Galileo and all those who have followed him are quite right there. There really is no place in the physical world for such extra properties. What we must say, rather, is that these properties are respectable, but *micro-physical*, properties of objects, surfaces, and so on.

The physical details are still in a good deal of confusion. The general idea is to find *micro-physical correlates* for the secondary qualities of physical objects and events and then to identify the qualities with these physical correlates. For instance, sounds will be identified with sound waves, or perhaps with the vibrating sources that cause these waves. Notice that this identification will be perfectly compatible with allowing that there can be *illusions* concerning these qualities, cases where the object appears to have, say, a certain colour, or seems to emit a certain sort of sound, but does not really have that colour or emit that sound. A perception of this sort would be no different from a thing looking to have a shape or a velocity that it does not have. Representation always allows the possibility of misrepresentation. But just what in detail these correlates are for particular sorts of perception has proved enormously hard to establish.

We cannot here discuss all the secondary qualities; so let us consider the particular case of colour, and even there restrict ourselves to the case of colour surfaces. We want to put colour on to the surfaces of things, where it seems to be, but we want to be good Materialists at the same time. We want to be *objective Materialists* about colours. (It is a fair choice of topic, because colours have given more trouble to objective Materialists than any other secondary quality.)

In my opinion, the most plausible theory along these lines is that advanced by David Hilbert in his short book *Color and Color Perception*, published in 1987. As well as being plausible, Hilbert's book is much easier to read than most other work on colour! (It contains, among other things, criticisms of things I have said about colour in the past, criticisms that seem to me to be pretty well conclusive. For criticism of Hilbert's view, based on empirical grounds drawn from facts about colour perception, see C. L. Hardin's article "Color and Illusion".)

We can perceive colours only because our retina contains three sorts of cone cells. The peak sensitivity of the three sorts is found within three different bands of the wave-lengths of the light that comes to the eye: the short, middle, and long waves. Hilbert argues that we are able with this apparatus, after processing the incoming stimuli in a sophisticated way, to pick up a quite complex property of the surface of objects. This property is called *surface spectral reflectance*. Here is what it is. As a result of light falling on the surface, called the *incident* light, light is reflected into the eye. Suppose we measure, for a particular wave-length, the *percentage* of the incident light that gets reflected by a certain point on the surface. Repeat this for each different wave-length falling on that point. You get a particular *percentage profile* for that point, which can be plotted on a graph. This is the surface spectral reflectance of the point. More strictly, it is a *triple* of reflectances, because the three sorts of cones each deliver their own particular reflectances. The triple, Hilbert claims, can be correlated with the colour of the surface at this point. This complex property is actually a physical disposition of the surface, although, of course, we are not aware of this in colour perception. Notice that all sorts of physically different surfaces can have the very same surface spectral reflectance. All that such surfaces have in common is the disposition to reflect incoming light according to this reflectance pattern. Hilbert argues that this disposition *is* the colour, the perceived colour, of the surface.

Notice that what we have here is *proportions* of the incident to the reflected light. We are not concerned with the *amount* of illumination that the surface receives. This explains colour-constancy, the fact that surfaces mostly look the same colour under different degrees of illumination. Reflectance is independent of illumination, that is, the amount of light falling on the surface. And since the property is a disposition, the surface, always provided it does not lose its particular physical nature, retains this property at all times, including in the dark. You cannot pick up the colour in the dark, but it is still there.

The system of colours, of course, has all sorts of relations holding within the system. Orange, for instance, 'lies between' red and yellow, and purple 'lies between' red and blue. The different hues form a circle. If a surface is one colour, it cannot at the same time have a different colour. Hilbert claims that these features can be explained in physical terms, given his reflectance theory.

There is a qualification to make. There are such things as *metamers*. These are different reflectance triples, which nevertheless yield exactly the same experienced colour. What this apparently forces the Materialist colour-objectivist to say is that surface colour is not simply one reflectance triple, but is rather a *disjunctive* disposition, the disjunction (this, or, this, or . . .) of all the reflectance triples that are linked with a particular shade of colour. (This will remind us of the point that Fodor made against type–type Materialism.) Hilbert actually has arguments to show that the metamer problem largely can be contained (See chap. 5 of his book). But in any case, a disjunction of causes should not create too much difficulty on the side of the perceiving subject. Different causes can bring about the same effect, that is, can make exactly the same neurons fire. All that needs to be admitted is that a disjunctive property is not a very impressive property. The Materialist colour-objectivist can live with this, I think. A reflectance triple possessed by a surface is a pretty unimportant, idiosyncratic property *from the physicist's point of view*. But, after all, lots of properties that are biologically important to us are in the same boat.

Robert Boyle compared the secondary qualities to keys that fit into locks in the person who perceives them. This analogy has often been mentioned by J.J.C. Smart in contemporary discussions. It is really quite helpful. The shape of the business end of a key is deliberately made to be a highly particular shape, so that it will open just one sort of lock. That shape is of no particular importance or interest for physical theory. But it is an objective material shape for all that. The secondary qualities are like that. (In the case of the metamers, though, to keep the analogy, you would have to have differently shaped keys all of which open the same lock.)

Galileo had the right idea in a way. The secondary qualities are not important physical properties. They do not carve the great beast of nature along any of its natural joints. The properties are ones that are merely important to us, and to other animals, because we are constructed so as to respond to them. Furthermore, patterns of surface reflectances, though 'out there', are not at all well correlated with the physical nature of the surface.

That means, though, that we are in rather urgent need of a story as to why we have evolved in this way. Why did this ability to detect surface spectral reflectance values get selected? Roger Shepard (1997) points out that, although different surface spectral reflectance is in itself unimportant, nevertheless it is, given natural illumination in the terrestrial environment (sunlight), an *invariant* property of the surface. As long as the surface is not physically changed, it will keep this complex property. This means that it can be used to *re-identify* objects. That is just what we use colours for. We can learn to identify edible fruits, say, by their characteristic colours and by the colours that they should have when they are ripe for eating. We can recognize individual persons, and other individual objects, by their particular pattern of colour surface. We can do this because these colours are more or less invariant. Surface spectral reflectance values are invariant in just the right way, and the eye (amazingly!) can pick up these reflectances.

11.3. Objections considered

So Hilbert, it seems, has given us a plausible objectivist and Materialist account of the nature of colours. Perhaps the same can be done for all the secondary qualities. It seems a promising programme. But some serious philosophical objections remain to be answered. The first one we should tackle is the problem already mentioned about aches, pains, itches, and tickles. Are they not sensations, and so mental, and do they not have special qualities attaching to them? What are we going to do about them?

In fact, however, we are rather ambiguous in our treatment of these phenomena. We readily enough agree that pain, for instance, is a sensation, and so is in the mind. At the same time, though, a doctor can ask us where the pain is, and we can tell him that it is in our hand. But if it is in our hand, it can hardly be in our mind. Aches, itches, and tickles are similarly 'doubly-located'.

We can deal with this somewhat puzzling situation if we think of having a pain, an itch, and so on as having a certain sort of perception. It is a species of *bodily* perception, which we have already discussed in Chapter 10. When we have a pain in our hand, we are perceiving that a certain sort of disturbance, a certain sort of bodily damage, is going on in our hand. The perception characteristically calls forth strong and stereotyped reactions—"I don't like this, something has to be done about it"—but it is essentially a perception. Like all perceptions, it can involve some error, as is shown when the doctor or dentist points out that the place where your pain feels to be is not the place where the damage actually is.

Given this account, we can argue plausibly that the special pain-quality is not a property of the sensation, that is, is not a property of the pain-perception but is a property of the *affected area of the body*. And then we can go on, just as in the case of the colours, to identify this property with some micro-physical happening at the place of the pain. Presumably it is stimulation of our pain-receptors. We then have dealt with the qualities involved in bodily sensations in just the same way that we have dealt with the traditional secondary qualities.

So far, so good. But we have still not dealt with the *phenomenological* objection. These micro-physical properties appear to be totally unlike the actual secondary qualities that we perceive. How can we be so naive as to think of identifying them? The verdict of perception seems clean against it! The secondary qualities, as we actually experience them, are simple or relatively simple. In particular, as Wilfrid Sellars argued, they lack any 'grain', that is to say, they lack complexity of structure at the observable level. The micro-physical properties with which it is proposed to identify them are complex structures, though, of course, minute structures. This is the Properties argument once again. The allegedly identical properties, say colours and reflectances, cannot be identical, because they themselves have properties, but, unfortunately, *different* properties from each other.

But what if secondary qualities such as colours were what I will call *gestalt* properties? The term is taken from the Gestalt psychologists but is not used in quite their sense. The idea is that the secondary qualities are micro-physical structural properties but are ones that we are able to grasp only in a *gestalt* or overall manner. Here is a model that begins, but no more than begins, to illustrate what is intended. Suppose that one is able to recognize that a number of quick showings of an extremely complex shape are showings of the very same shape again; suppose one picks this shape out quite reliably from other similar shapes; but suppose also that one is unable to analyze the shape to any great degree or say what the difference from other shapes consisted in. "They just seem different, that is all." This situation is clearly possible, and our recognition of 'that shape again' would have a 'gestalt' quality. We would 'get' the shape but be unable to analyze it; we would be unable to perceive its detailed structure. In this shape case, of course, we would be aware that it was *shapes* that we were dealing with. But why should there not be visual properties that are *totally* impenetrable to visual analysis, so that in the state of nature we had no clue at all to micro-structure, or even that the property had a micro-structure? My suggestion is that our visual apprehension of colour is like that.

There are some people who find this suggestion incredible. I have two suggestions about why they might find it so, despite it being (as I hope) true. The *first* reason is this. We have a great tendency to think that we have a *through and through* awareness of the sensible qualities (whether primary or secondary). We think that we grasp them in their whole nature, and that they therefore can have no hidden depths in them.

Mark Johnston (1997, p. 138) has drawn attention to a passage in Bertrand Russell that is a wonderful example of this idea. Russell wrote:

> The particular shade of colour that I am seeing ... may have many things to be said about it. ... But such statements, though they may make me know truths *about* the colour, do not make me know the colour itself any better than I did before: so far as concerns knowledge of the colour itself, as opposed to knowledge of truths about it, I know the colour perfectly and completely when I see it, and no further knowledge of it is even theoretically possible. (1912, pp. 73–74)

It is clear, I think, where Russell's assumption comes from. It starts from the Cartesian–Humean idea that mental entities, and our perceptions in particular, are known through and through, and without any possibility of error. Since Russell thinks of colour as in the mind, he is sure that he knows colours through and through, and without any possibility of error.

Against this, I would once again advance the idea (it was already advanced in our discussion of Descartes) that everything in the world, *everything*, every event, every property of things and events, every relation that things and events have to each other, are each one of them an epistemological *iceberg*. Our knowledge and rational belief about all these things, though real, is selective and limited. If you take this view then it becomes much easier to accept that the secondary qualities might have hidden depths to which we cannot penetrate in perception. Hilbert, by the way, is very much aware of this point in defending his objective Materialism about colour and says that to reason in this way, in Descartes' way, in Russell's way, is to commit 'the fallacy of total information'.

One great philosopher who rejected the fallacy of total information in connection with the sensible qualities, and whose authority I now add to that of Hilbert's, was Leibniz. He argues for this in a number of places in his great commentary on Locke. Writing about Locke's remark that there is no resemblance between pain and the motion of a piece of steel dividing our flesh, Leibniz replies:

> It is true that pain does not resemble the movement of a pin; but it might thoroughly resemble the motions which the pin causes in our body, and might represent them in the soul; and I have not the least doubt that it does. That is why we say the pain is in our body and not in the pin, although we say that the light is in the fire; because there are motions in the fire which the senses cannot clearly detect individually, but which form a confusion—a running together—which is brought within the reach of the senses and is represented to us by the idea of light. (*New Essays on Human Understanding*, p. 132)

Again, "The ideas . . . of sensible qualities retain their place among the simple ideas only because of our ignorance" (p. 170).

These views of Leibniz have, strangely enough, received almost no publicity. It is no accident at all that Leibniz was, unlike almost everybody else until fairly recently, the great early critic of Descartes' doctrine of the utter transparency of consciousness to itself.

So, against those who find the suggestion incredible that the secondary qualities are nothing but micro-physical properties of objects inadequately apprehended, it has been argued that it is much easier to accept this view if we give up the idea that these qualities are things that, in Berkeley's seductive phrase, 'we perfectly know'.

But it is not just Cartesian fallacies about the mind that may lead us to embrace the fallacy of total information. There is also the illusion that earlier in this book (3.1) was called 'the Headless Woman illusion'. In the state of nature, we certainly have no notion that the secondary qualities are micro-physical primary properties. The identification, supposing it to be correct, is made on theoretical, not observational, grounds. In perception, we are not aware of this identity. It will be quite natural, then, as the Headless Woman illusion shows in the setting of a conjuring trick, to pass from this lack of awareness of identity to a strong impression that these qualities are *not* identical with the relevant micro-physical properties. This, then, is another source of the fallacious impression that the identification must be wrong.

If this is the correct theory of our perceptions of sensible qualities, then it should extend without too much difficulty to other mental phenomena insofar as we are aware of them. The having of mental images, for instance, including memory images, will be representings that resemble perceptions but are subtly different from them. But these important details must be left aside here.

11.4. Perceptions of qualities are representations

So now let us bring this discussion of the qualia to a conclusion. If the line of thought that I have been following out is correct, then the sensible qualities—and in particular the secondary qualities—are, none of them, in the mind when we perceive. What *is* in the mind? Simply *representations* of things in the world. Objects are represented as having certain qualities (and standing in certain relations to each other). Of course, these representations must not be thought of as little pictures of the world. The resemblances involved in *picturing* would bring qualities back into the mind, starting up the whole problem again. A perception of something red is not coloured, the smelling of something smelly does not itself have a smell.[1]

What is in the mind when we perceive must be some exceedingly abstract structure that maps rather than pictures the world. If a Materialism about the mind is to be defended, the structure must be so abstract that it can somehow be encoded in purely physical tissue, in the neurons of our brain.

Representations of reality can be false as well as true. In sensory illusion, still more in hallucinatory experience, we have false representations. What is the status of the 'things represented', the apparent bentness of the oar half in water, the things that appear to be going on in hallucinations (and dreams)? The old 'sense-datum' theory of perception insisted that these things did have a reality, but not an ordinary physical reality. Some philosophers still hold to this view. *But a Materialist must deny this.* The representations exist as physical encodings, as represent*ings* in a purely physical brain. But the things represent*ed* do not exist at all! The oar is there, but it is not bent, and there is no substitute object that is bent. The hallucinatory scene, and the dream scene, do not exist either. This is an important part of the defence of an objectivist (or as some say, Direct Realist) account of the secondary qualities.

11.5. Introspective consciousness revisited

It may perhaps help to understand the position that has been defended here if we go back to the topic of introspective consciousness, taken up in the last chapter. I think that many philosophers think that the view I have been defending in this chapter can pretty much be refuted simply by 'turning our gaze into our own breast', that is by introspecting. Here is a suggestion about why such philosophers are so sure that my sort of view is wrong.

In the chapter on Eliminativism, at 8.3, I gave a brief exposition of Wilfrid Sellars' distinction between the 'manifest' and the 'scientific' image of the world. Scientific Realists such as myself think that the 'image' of the world that we gain through ordinary, unscientific experience must give way to a truer, much less familiar, image of the world that the natural sciences, and in particular physics, is gradually building up for us. There is, of course, a limit to this process of rubbishing the manifest image, because it is evidence that comes to us from our senses that supports the rape of our senses by scientific theory. But the manifest image of the world, we scientific Realists think, can be no more than a first stab at understanding the nature of physical reality. All this is perhaps difficult, but is now fairly familiar.

But what of the quasi-sensory access each of has to our own mind that we gain in introspection? Philosophers, I suggest, even scientific Realists, have not fully and inwardly realized that the same distinction that we draw in the case of perception between manifest and scientific image should be drawn in the case of introspection. I would put it by saying that philosophers have been unable to shake off the old—and, I have already argued, false—Cartesian doctrine that the mind is first and best known. In this way, philosophers conclude that because the mental appears to them a certain way, that is the way it must be.

Colin McGinn, in an interesting but defeatist article, "Can We Solve the Mind–Body Problem?", says:

> Our acquaintance with consciousness could hardly be more direct; phenomenological description thus comes (relatively) easy. "Introspection" is the name of the faculty through which we catch consciousness in all its vivid nakedness. . . . We thus have 'immediate' access to the properties of consciousness. (pp. 7–8)

That word 'nakedness' reeks of Cartesian epistemology. Consider the following parody:

> Perception is the name of the faculty in which we catch the physical world in all its vivid nakedness. . . . We thus have 'immediate access' to the properties of the physical world

Scientific Realists will surely reject the latter. Equally, I say, a scientific Realist ought to reject what McGinn says about introspection. If we do reject this way of thinking about introspection, we shall find it easier to accept that when we introspect, what we are introspecting are some of our own brain processes, brain processes that *represent*. The content of our awareness, of course, is restricted to an awareness of what these processes represent. We then find it easy, in our philosophizing, to confuse these representations with the things represented—qualities and such. I have already remarked how easy that particular confusion is for human beings.

11.6. Note to Chapter 11

The line of thought that I have been following out here would, of course, be rejected by a number of philosophers. They think that the secondary qualities just have to be qualities over and above those recognized by physical science. The most important and persuasive defence of this view has come from Frank Jackson, originally in an article titled "Epiphenomenal Qualia", already mentioned during our discussion of Thomas Huxley's position. Jackson's argument for qualia, which he calls the 'Knowledge argument', involves the imaginary case of Mary, a brilliant scientist who knows everything physical that there is to know about colour. Unfortunately for her, however, she has never seen any colours. She has spent her life in a room where everything visible in it is black or white, including the screen of the TV that gives her access to the world. Then one day she is released and sees colours for the first time. Jackson argues that this seeing of colours gives Mary *new knowledge* and that this new knowledge must be knowledge of further qualities, over and above her scientific knowledge.

The argument has been widely supported and widely rejected, although just how it is to be rejected is a matter of dispute. Jackson restated his position against objections in "What Mary Didn't Know" (1986). In Braddon-Mitchell and Jackson's introductory text, *Philosophy of Mind and Cognition* (1996), the argument, and replies to it, are discussed again (pp. 127–135). By that time, however, Jackson's attitude to the argument had become: There must be a good answer to the Knowledge argument, but it is not clear what it is.

My own answer has already been presented in the body of this chapter. The 'new' qualities that Mary perceives are in fact microphysical properties, but they are not perceived as such. They are perceived, instead, in a 'gestalt' way that cannot, in perception, penetrate to their deeper, micro-physical nature. She does get new experiences, because previously she knew only about that deeper nature. (She worked the other way round from us.) But only in some stretched sense is it new knowledge.

Notes

1. See the remarkable paper "Experience" by B. A. Farrell, published, somewhat amazingly, back in 1950.

Readings and references for the sensible qualities

Berkeley, George. 1713. "First Dialogue Between Hylas and Philonous." In *Berkeley's Philosophical Writings*, ed. David M. Armstrong. New York, Collier-Macmillan, 1965.
Block, Ned, Owen Flanagan, and Güven Güzeldere, eds. 1997. *The Nature of Consciousness*. Cambridge, Mass.: MIT Press, A Bradford Book. See sections VII, VIII, and IX. An extensive collection of readings.

Braddon-Mitchell, David, and Frank Jackson. 1996. *Philosophy of Mind and Cognition*. Oxford: Blackwell.

Burtt, E. A. 1954. *The Metaphysical Foundations of Modern Physical Science*. New York: Doubleday Anchor Books.

Byrne, Alex, and David R. Hilbert, eds. 1997. *Readings on Color*. Vol. 1, *The Philosophy of Color;* Vol. 2, *The Science of Color*. Cambridge, Mass.: MIT Press, Bradford Books. For those who wish to get to grips with the full intricacy of the topic of colour.

Campbell, Keith. 1993. "David Armstrong and Realism About Colour." In *Ontology, Causality, and Mind*, ed. John Bacon, Keith Campbell, and Lloyd Reinhardt, pp. 249–268. Cambridge: Cambridge University Press. Criticizes Armstrong's theory and gives important references on colour. Armstrong replies on pages 268–273.

Chalmers, David. 1996. *The Conscious Mind*. New York and Oxford: Oxford University Press. Presents, with great verve and brilliance, a view on the question of qualia that is directly opposed to the one defended in this chapter.

Churchland, P. M. 1985. "Reduction, Qualia, and the Direct Inspection of Brain States." *Journal of Philosophy* 82: pp. 8–28. A reply to Frank Jackson's Knowledge argument.

Farrell, B. A. 1950. "Experience." *Mind* 50: 170–198.

Hardin, C. L. 1990. "Color and Illusion." In *Mind and Cognition*, ed. W. G. Lycan, pp. 555–567. Cambridge, Mass.: Blackwell. Argues against the views of Armstrong, Smart, Lewis, Averill, and Hilbert on empirical grounds drawn from colour perception.

Hilbert, David R. 1987. *Color and Color Perception: A Study in Anthropocentric Realism*, Stanford: CSLI. An important and clearly written defence of an objectivist and Physicalist theory of colour.

Horgan, T. 1984. "Jackson on Physical Information and Qualia." *Philosophical Quarterly* 34: pp. 147–155. A reply to Jackson's Knowledge argument.

Jackson, Frank. 1982. "Epiphenomenal Qualia." *Philosophical Quarterly* 30: pp. 147–155. It is reprinted in Lycan's *Mind and Cognition*.

_____. 1986. "What Mary Didn't Know." *Journal of Philosophy* 83: pp. 291–295. Replies to critics of the Knowledge argument.

Johnston, Mark. 1997. "How to Speak of the Colours." In *Readings on Color*. Vol. 1, *The Philosophy of Color*, ed. Alex Byrne and David R. Hilbert, pp. 137–176. Cambridge, Mass.: MIT Press, A Bradford Book. Reprinted from *Philosophical Studies* 68 (1992): pp. 221–263.

Leibniz, G. W. 1765. *New Essays on Human Understanding*, trans. and ed. Peter Remnant and Jonathan Bennett. Cambridge: Cambridge University Press, 1981.

Lewis, David. 1990. "What Experience Teaches." In Lycan, *Mind and Cognition*, pp. 499–518. A reply to Jackson's Knowledge argument. Further material is in *Mind and Cognition*, section 17.

Lycan, William G. 1990. *Mind and Cognition.*, Cambridge, Mass.: Blackwell.

———. 1996. *Consciousness and Experience*. Cambridge, Mass.: MIT Press, A Bradford Book. Defends, among other things, an objectivist and Materialist account of the secondary qualities. Lycan's position on the mind–body problem is closer to mine than, I think, any other philosopher of mind. I have learnt much from him.

McGinn, Colin. 1991. "Can We Solve the Mind–Body Problem?" Chap. 1 in *The Problem of Consciousness*. Oxford: Blackwell.

Russell, Bertrand. 1912. *The Problems of Philosophy*. London: Thornton Butterworth, Home University Library.

Shepard, Roger N. 1997. "The Perceptual Organization of Colors: An Adaptation to Regularities of the Terrestrial World?" In *The Philosophy of Color*. Vol. 2, *The Science of Color*, ed. Alex Byrne and David R. Hilbert, pp. 311–356. Cambridge, Mass.: MIT Press, A Bradford Book.

Tye, Michael. 1995. *Ten Problems of Consciousness*. Cambridge, Mass.: MIT Press, A Bradford Book. Defends, like Lycan and me, an objectivist and Materialist account of the secondary qualities. Offers as a slogan: "Qualia ain't in the head".

CHAPTER TWELVE

Intentionality

A text for this chapter is Tim Crane's The Mechanical Mind, *in particular chapter 5.*

The argument of the last two chapters has been that introspective consciousness is a representation of (some of) the current contents of our own mind. A teleological-biological explanation has been given of why we have this faculty: it is to enable us to plan inside our heads. Perception we have seen as first-order representation, a representation of the current state of our environment and our body. When we have introspective awareness of our own perceptions, we have higher-order representations, representations of our first-order representations.

But what is it for a mind to represent? And is such representing, particularly the sophisticated representing that human beings are able to do, compatible with Materialism and the 'Physicalist dream'? That is the final problem that we take up in this book.

12.1. The Hegemony of Representation

I begin by advancing a hypothesis that is perhaps not essential to the Materialist programme but that, if true, would be a most useful preliminary simplification. This the doctrine that Bill Lycan calls, rather grandiloquently, 'the Hegemony of Representation'. He defines the doctrine in this way: "The mind has no special properties that are not exhausted by its representational properties, along with or in combination with the functional organization of its components" (*Consciousness and Experience*, p. 11).

Perception is representational: That seems straightforward enough. It is also quite plausible that bodily sensation is bodily perception. I have already argued in Chapter 10 that introspective awareness is representational. Knowledge, belief, and thought are, fairly clearly, representational. Mental imagery is a bit more tricky, perhaps. But suppose you summon up an image of something green. This summoning is rather like perception, as many philosophers and others have noticed, even though, unlike perception, imaging is to some extent under the direct control of the will. Are we not representing some green thing (a physical thing, although it need not be any particular physical thing)? Or perhaps we are representing the *seeing* of some green thing, a representing that would involve introspective consciousness.

What of purposes, intentions, impulses, and desires? They still seem to be representative in nature, although here we are representing the world as we want it to be rather than how we take it to be. Finally, the emotions seem to be complex mental structures involving desires, impulses, beliefs, and bodily sensations. So the Hegemony of Representation looks to be a plausible enough view. Note, however, as Lycan does, that although the mental is always a matter of representation, there might be representations that we do not want to class as mental. For instance, we might want to say that our genes encode information, and thus contain representations in some sense, without thinking that genes have a mental side to them.

12.2. Analyzing intentionality

Instead of the term 'representation' the usual technical term used by philosophers is 'inten*t*ionality'. The term goes right back to the Scholastic philosophers in the Middle Ages. It is unfortunate that there is another term, 'inten*s*ionality', that it is easily confused with. It is actually quite hard to say the two words in such a way that the difference between the 't' and the 's' is clear to one's hearer. You pretty well have to say 'intentionality-with-a-t' and 'intensionality-with-an-s'. Fortunately, however, we won't be further concerned with intensionality here. (Intensionality is a property of *sentences*. A clear account of it is to be found in Tim Crane's *The Mechanical Mind*, pp. 32–37, which is in any case a useful book for this chapter.)

A key feature of an intentional state, or a representation, is that it points beyond itself, that it is 'about' something, but that the something it is about need not exist. A perception points to some state of affairs, but that state of affairs need not exist. If it does not exist, then we have illusory or hallucinatory perception. A person's desire for a drink points beyond itself to that person drinking. But the desire need not be fulfilled, that is, the drinking may not be forthcoming. And so for all intentional states. This leads to an important consequence. What makes an intentional state intentional, what makes it representational, is not a *relation* to what is often called its *content*, that is, the thing it points to, or is about. For a relation demands (or so it would be generally agreed—there are a few philosophers who differ) that all its terms exist.

This seems to make intentionality both special and mysterious. Does it not require a special sort of thing to point beyond itself in this manner? Could mere matter, however organized, do this? The Austrian philosopher, Franz Brentano, who flourished at the end of the last century, was so impressed by the intentionality of the mind that he thought that it was the special mark of the mental. The mental is intentional, nothing material is intentional, so mind and matter are perfectly distinct. In effect, he used a Properties argument to show the difference of mind from matter. The Materialist has to meet this challenge.

It seems that Brentano went too fast, though. There are properties of ordinary physical things that exhibit just this pointing beyond themselves to events that may never exist. We have already met with such properties in this book. They are *dispositions*. The analogy between dispositions (more generally, the powers of things) and the intentional nature of mental states was, as far as I know, first pointed out in an unpublished paper by John Burnheim at Sydney University but was first argued in detail by C. B. Martin and K. Pfeifer in a paper titled "Intentionality and the Non-Psychological" (1986).

Consider the brittleness of a glass. Its brittleness ensures that if it is sharply struck, then it will shatter. That it actually shatters as a result of being sharply struck is the manifestation of the brittleness. But, of course, the manifestation may never occur. The result is that the brittleness of the glass stands to the manifestation of brittleness in the same sort of relation that an intentional state stands to its intentional object. Both point to an object or state of affairs that need not exist. You will remember that Ryle made great use of dispositions in his attempt to elucidate the concept of mind. But if dispositions already have proto-intentionality, a primitive sort of intentionality, then we Materialists can try to give an account of intentionality in terms of the dispositions bestowed upon us by the material brain.

It was argued, of course, that Ryle's own account of dispositions was not satisfactory and that we do best to think of dispositions as actual inner states of the disposed object. But that will do a central-state Materialist just fine. It is also clear that the dispositions involved in the mental are far, far more complex and sophisticated than those possessed by a mere piece of glass. But it seems that an account of intentionality that looks to the dispositional may be on the right track.

12.3. A simple case analyzed

In thinking about intentionality, some things look relatively simple and easy (*relatively* only!); others look hard. Consider a problem that Wittgenstein poses in his *Philosophical Investigations*. At 177e he asks: "What makes my image of him [a friend, say] into an image of HIM?" It is a quite sketchy image, and let us say it is a friend that you have not seen for years. Yet there is no question about who you are imaging. The intentionality, the person who the image represents, is not in doubt. But what dispositions, or whatever, can you point to? This case is one of the hard ones. So it seems that we should start with something simpler and hope to work up, now or in the future. That is generally how progress is made in inquiry. If you could just solve the intentionality problem for lizards, you would be doing quite a good job! This difficulty suggests that we ought to start with perceptions and with simple purposes, purposes related to the things we perceive in our environment.

Let us then start with colour perception and with the perception of something red. The intentional object of our perception will be a state of affairs: Something over there is red. (Remember that I am assuming that redness is an objective micro-physical property. The argument should go through without this assumption, but let us ignore such a complication.) The following mechanism exists in creatures that can perceive colours, including the colour red. The object acts causally on our eyes and, provided other conditions are suitable (roughly, in normal conditions), the perceiver will have a perception that the object is red. The perception is some sort of neural registration in the brain apt for being caused by a red thing. This registration will then *empower* (dispose) the perceiver in a certain way. *If the perceiver should so purpose*, the perceiver can act physically in some way that picks this red thing out from other things, in particular from things that are not red, either things that have another colour or have no colour at all. It is helpful here to think of the discrimination experiments that psychologists design both for human beings and for other animals. Suppose there are a number of passages. At any one time, one passage and one only displays a red card above it. If an animal can be trained to select the red passage for some reward, then, given various experimental controls, this suggests that it is reacting to the red card as a *red* card.

What we have here may be called a *causal circuit*. The circuit begins in the object and goes from there to the effect in the perceiver's brain. The second half of the circuit may not occur, but at least the perceiver must have the capacity to react to the red object *as* a red object. If the second half does occur, we can say that the circuit is *closed*. But all that is essential to the perceiving is the capacity, or power, or disposition, to close the circuit, reacting, as it were, under the guidance of the redness of the object. But the 'guidance' is a purely causal affair.

This capacity to close such a causal circuit is, of course, an evolutionary affair, developed, as naturalists think, by natural selection. If this is so, is it not reasonable to say that this is what this mechanism is *for*, in the biological sense? The mechanism developed just because it allowed red-discrimination. And, further, can we not say that the neural registration is *a perception of something red*, having as its intentional object the state of affairs: the object's being red? Where the same neural registration occurs but its cause is not a red object, its intentional object will be the same, but it will be a *merely* intentional object. The perception will be a mis-perception.

Having said all this, the next thing to say is that, as it stands, the account is much too crude. The first thing to notice is that in giving an account of what it is to perceive something red, it was necessary to bring *purposes* into the analysis. The red-selective behaviour that closes the causal circuit will have to be purposive behaviour, a course of action that has some aim. What this shows is a point that has already been mentioned when discussing the Causal theory of the mind. Perception and purposes form a package deal, so that you cannot have one without the other. It is easy enough to see that purposive behaviour in the environment will be impossible without continuing perception of that environment, right up to the perception that 'switches off' the purpose because it has been achieved. (And we can identify the content of that last perception with the intentional object of the purpose.) But we have now also seen that perception seems to need the capacity for purposive action of a selective sort. So we get the two-way connection.

This leads on to the second, still more radical, sophistication. Purposive behaviour, except for the simplest of actions, involves courses of action, such as going through a passage that has a red card above it. Courses of action, however, involve a whole succession of perceptions. Purposes also, even quite simple purposes, involve adapting means to ends, which means that they will regularly involve subpurposes: the purpose to carry out the sub-purposes as means to the larger purpose. What this means, I think, is that perceptions and purposes do not come singly. They are like soldiers and armies. Without quite a number of soldiers (just how many is an essentially vague matter) you do not have an army, and until you have an army you do not have even a single soldier. Quite a complicated package deal. Perceptions and purposes are like this. Without at least the capacity for a *range* of perceptions and a *range* of purposes, you do not have any perceptions or purposes at all. And it will be an essentially vague matter just how considerable the two ranges must be before we can attribute even this, the lowest grade of mentality. The vagueness is an advantage, I think. No Materialist would want there to be anything but a somewhat vague line between living things that lack mentality and living things that have mentality.

12.4. Going beyond simple intentionalities

Perhaps this analysis has taken us as far as the lizard, which you may think is not far. But it is a pretty good beginning, I think. For to give this account of our perception of the sensible qualities (and relations) is to give an account of the fundamental concepts involved in our sensory interaction with the environment. This account must lie at the centre of the intentionality problem. Everything else, we can hope, will be a further sophistication built on this.

How are we to go on? Given *any* mental representation, for instance the image of my friend, we want to say what it is for it to represent. That is the intentionality problem. Broadly, two approaches have been tried. The first is a causal approach. What a representation represents is, or is connected with, is what brings that representation into existence. You can see at once that theories of this sort are going to have the most serious problems with representations that represent the nonexistent, which has few, if any, causal powers!

The other approach is the behavioural approach. What determines what our beliefs and what our desires are is determined by the way that we are impelled to act. The view was put in a vivid way by the Cambridge philosopher Frank Ramsey, who said that a belief that everybody in Cambridge voted is 'a map of neigbouring space by which we steer' ("General Propositions and Causality", p. 146). A complication here that Ramsey does not address is that we may steer differently, that is, behave differently, given the same belief but different desires.

For the case of elementary perceptions, that is, the perception that some object in the environment has certain sensible qualities, I have argued that you have both a causal and a behavioural element. We need causes acting on the perceiver and causes produced by the perceiver, the latter being the behaviour. The perception that something is red is characteristically caused by a red surface. It also endows the perceiver with a capacity to react back towards a surface in a way that discriminates between the surface and something that is not red, if the perceiver is both willing and able. This complex *causal role* (David Lewis's phrase) gets the best of both sorts of theory. The perception is the effect of a certain sort of cause and the cause of certain sorts of effect. We can add to this the teleological element: what this causal role is *for* in the biological sense.

But for more sophisticated sorts of mental representation, cases where we get far beyond the lizard, it seems to me that the behaviour (capacity for behaviour) is much more important than the cause. I don't really know how to go on, so I will leave the matter here. But for those who do want to go further, an ideal introduction is chapter 5 of Tim Crane's *The Mechanical Mind*, which also gives full references. Crane makes it clear that the Materialist has quite a way to go before 'showing how intentionality is possible' for a purely material being.

Readings and references for intentionality

Armstrong, D. M. 1993. *A Materialist Theory of the Mind*. London: Routledge. See chapter 11, section V, "The Intentionality of Perception".

Crane, Tim. 1995. *The Mechanical Mind*. London: Penguin Books.

Lycan, William G. 1996. *Consciousness and Experience*. Cambridge, Mass.: MIT Press, A Bradford Book.

Martin C. B., and K. Pfeifer. 1986. "Intentionality and the Non-Psychological." *Philosophy and Phenomenological Research* 46: pp. 277–289.

Ramsey, Frank. 1990. "General Propositions and Causality." In *Philosophical Papers: F. P. Ramsey*, ed. D. H. Mellor, pp. 145–163. Cambridge: Cambridge University Press.

Sterelny, Kim. 1990. *The Representational Theory of Mind: An Introduction*. Oxford: Blackwell. To be recommended. An introductory book that begins about where this book ends.

Wittgenstein, Ludwig. 1953. *Philosophical Investigations*. Trans. G.E.M. Anscombe. Oxford: Blackwell.

"ON THE HYPOTHESIS THAT ANIMALS ARE AUTOMATA, AND ITS HISTORY" BY THOMAS HUXLEY [1874]

This paper is taken from Thomas Huxley, Methods and Results, vol. 1 of Collected Essays (London: Macmillan and Co., 1893). The article is very long, so I have omitted substantial portions, without, I hope, destroying the beautifully clear and careful way in which Huxley deploys his argument. The same numbers that are used in the first half of this book's Chapter 4 have been inserted, so that Huxley's text can be correlated with my exposition of it. All omissions are marked . . . .

[4.1.1]

The first half of the seventeenth century is one of the great epochs of biological science. For though suggestions and indications of the conceptions which took definite shape, at that time, are to be met with in works of earlier date, they are little more than the shadows which coming truth casts forward; men's knowledge was neither extensive enough, nor exact enough, to show them the solid body of fact which threw these shadows.

But, in the seventeenth century, the idea that the physical processes of life are capable of being explained in the same way as other physical phenomena, and, therefore, that the living body is a mechanism, was proved to be true for certain classes of vital actions; and, having thus taken firm root in irrefragable fact, this conception has not only successfully repelled every assault which has been made upon it, but has steadily grown in force and extent of application, until it is now the expressed or implied fundamental proposition of the whole doctrine of scientific Physiology.

If we ask to whom mankind are indebted for this great service, the general voice will name William Harvey. For, by his discovery of the circulation of the blood in the higher animals, by his explanation of the nature of the mechanism by which that circulation is effected, and by his no less remarkable, though less known, investigations of the process of development, Harvey solidly laid the foundations of all those physical explanations of the functions of sustentation and reproduction which modern physiologists have achieved.

But the living body is not only sustained and reproduced: it adjusts itself to external and internal changes; it moves and feels. The attempt to reduce the endless complexities of animal motion and feeling to law and order is, at least, as important a part of the task of the physiologist as the elucidation of what are sometimes called the vegetative processes. Harvey did not make this attempt himself; but the influence of his work upon the man who did make it is patent and unquestionable. This man was René Descartes, who, though by many years Harvey's junior, died before him; and yet in his short span of fifty-four years, took an undisputed place, not only among the chiefs of philosophy, but amongst the greatest and most original of mathematicians; while, in my belief, he is no less certainly entitled to the rank of a great and original physiologist; inasmuch as he did for the physiology of motion and sensation that which Harvey had done for the circulation of the blood, and opened up that road to the mechanical theory of these processes, which has been followed by all his successors.

Descartes was no mere speculator, as some would have us believe: but a man who knew of his own knowledge what was to be known of the facts of anatomy and physiology in his day. He was an unwearied dissector and observer; and it is said, that, on a visitor once asking to see his library, Descartes led him into a room set aside for dissections, and full of specimens under examination. "There," said he, "is my library." . . .

[4.1.2]

... I shall now endeavour to show that a series of propositions, which constitute the foundation and essence of the modern physiology of the nervous system, are fully expressed and illustrated in the works of Descartes.

I. The brain is the organ of sensation, thought, and emotion; that is to say, some change in the condition of the matter of this organ is the invariable antecedent of the state of consciousness to which each of these terms is applied.

In the " Principes de la Philosophie" (§ 169), Descartes says:

> Although the soul is united to the whole body, its principal functions are, nevertheless, performed in the brain; it is here that it not only understands and imagines, but also feels; and this is effected by the intermediation of the nerves, which extend in the form of delicate threads from the brain to all parts of the body, to which they are attached in such a manner, that we can hardly touch any part of the body without setting the extremity of some nerve in motion. This motion passes along the nerve to that part of the brain which is the common sensorium, as I have sufficiently explained in my 'Treatise on Dioptrics'; and the movements which thus travel along the nerves, as far as that part of the brain with which the soul is closely joined and united, cause it, by reason of their diverse characters, to have different thoughts. And it is those different thoughts of the soul, which arise immediately from the movements that are excited by the nerves in the brain, which we properly term our feelings, or the perceptions of our senses.

Elsewhere, Descartes, in arguing that the seat of the passions is not (as many suppose) the heart, but the brain, uses the following remarkable language:

> The opinion of those who think that the soul receives its passions in the heart, is of no weight, for it is based upon the fact that the passions cause a change to be felt in that organ; and it is easy to see that this change is felt, as if it were in the heart, only by the intermediation of a little nerve which descends from the brain to it; just as pain is felt, as if it were in the foot; by the intermediation of the nerves of the foot; and the stars are perceived, as if they were in the heavens, by the

intermediation of their light and of the optic nerves. So that it is no more necessary for the soul to exert its functions immediately in the heart, to feel its passions there, than it is necessary that it should be in the heavens to see the stars there.

This definite allocation of all the phenomena of consciousness to the brain as their organ, was a step the value of which it is difficult for us to appraise, so completely has Descartes' view incorporated itself with everyday thought and common language. A lunatic is said to be "crack-brained" or "touched in the head", a confused thinker is "muddle-headed", while a clever man is said to have "plenty of brains"; but it must be remembered that at the end of the last century a considerable, though much over-estimated, anatomist, Bichat, so far from having reached the level of Descartes, could gravely argue that the apparatuses of organic life are the sole seat of the passions, which in no way affect the brain, except so far as it is the agent by which the influence of the passions is transmitted to the muscles.

Modern physiology, aided by pathology, easily demonstrates that the brain is the seat of all forms of consciousness, and fully bears out Descartes' explanation of the reference of those sensations in the viscera which accompany intense emotion, to these organs. It proves, directly, that those states of consciousness which we call sensations are the immediate consequent of a change in the brain excited by the sensory nerves; and, on the well-known effects of injuries, of stimulants, and of narcotics, it bases the conclusion that thought and emotion are, in like manner, the consequents of physical antecedents.

II. The movements of animals are due to the change of form of muscles, which shorten and become thicker; and this change of form in a muscle arises from a motion of the substance contained within the nerves which go to the muscle.

In the "Passions de l'âme" [The Passions of the Soul] Art. vii., Descartes writes:

> Moreover; we know that all the movements of the limbs depend on the muscles, and that these muscles are opposed to one another in such a manner, that when one of them shortens, it draws along the part of the body to which it is attached, and so gives rise to a simultaneous elongation of the muscle which is opposed to it. Then, if it

happens, afterwards, that the latter shortens, it causes the former to
elongate, and draws towards itself the part to which it is attached.
Lastly, we know that all these movements of the muscles, as all the
senses, depend on the nerves, which are like little threads or tubes,
which all come from the brain, and, like it, contain a certain very subtle air or wind, termed the animal spirits.

The property of muscle mentioned by Descartes now goes by the
general name of contractility, but his definition of it remains untouched. . . .

*III. The sensations of animals are due to a motion of the substance
of the nerves which connect the sensory organs with the brain.*

In "La Dioptrique" (Fourth Discourse), Descartes explains, more
fully than in the passage cited above, his hypothesis of the mode of
action of sensory nerves:

It is the little threads of which the inner substance of the nerves is
composed which subserve sensation. You must conceive that these
little threads, being enclosed in tubes, which are always distended
and kept open by the animal spirits which they contain, neither press
upon nor interfere with one another and are extended from the brain
to the extremities of all the members which are sensitive—in such a
manner, that the slightest touch which excites the part of one of the
members to which a thread is attached, gives rise to a motion of the
part of the brain whence it arises, just as by pulling one of the ends of
a stretched cord, the other end is instantaneously moved. . . . And we
must take care not to imagine that, in order to feel, the soul needs to
behold certain images sent by the objects of sense to the brain, as our
philosophers commonly suppose; or, at least, we must conceive these
images to be something quite different from what they suppose them
to be. For, as all they suppose is that these images ought to resemble
the objects which they represent, it is impossible for them to show
how they can be formed by the objects received by the organs of the
external senses and transmitted to the brain. And they have had no
reason for supposing the existence of these images except this; seeing
that the mind is readily excited by a picture to conceive the object
which is depicted, they have thought that it must be excited in the
same way to conceive those objects which affect our senses by little
pictures of them formed in the head; instead of which we ought to
recollect that there are many things besides images which may excite

the mind, as, for example, signs and words, which have not the least resemblance to the objects which they signify.[1]

Modern physiology amends Descartes' conception of the mode of action of sensory nerves in detail, by showing that their structure is the same as that of motor nerves; and that the changes which take place in them, when the sensory organs with which they are connected are excited, are of just the same nature as those which occur in motor nerves, when the muscles to which they are distributed are made to contract: there is a molecular change which, in the case of the sensory nerve, is propagated towards the brain. But the great fact insisted upon by Descartes, that no likeness of external things is, or can be, transmitted to the mind by the sensory organs; on the contrary, that, between the external cause of a sensation and the sensation, there is interposed a mode of motion of nervous matter, of which the state of consciousness is no likeness, but a mere symbol, is of the profoundest importance. . . .

[4.1.3]

For of two alternatives one must be true. Either consciousness is the function of a something distinct from the brain, which we call the soul, and a sensation is the mode in which this soul is affected by the motion of a part of the brain; or there is no soul, and a sensation is something generated by the mode of motion of a part of the brain. In the former case, the phenomena of the senses are purely spiritual affections; in the latter, they are something manufactured by the mechanism of the body, and as unlike the causes which set that mechanism in motion, as the sound of a repeater is unlike the pushing of the spring which gives rise to it. . . .

[4.1.4]

IV. The motion of the matter of a sensory nerve may be transmitted through the brain to motor nerves, and thereby give rise to contraction of the muscles to which these motor nerves are distributed; and this reflection of motion from a sensory into a motor nerve may take place without volition, or even contrary to it.

In stating these important truths, Descartes defined that which we now term "reflex action." Indeed he almost uses the term itself, as he talks of the "animal spirits" as " réfléchis"[2], from the sensory into the motor nerves. . . .

Nothing can be clearer in statement, or in illustration, than the view of reflex action which Descartes gives in the "The Passions of the Soul", Art. xiii. After recapitulating the manner in which sensory impressions transmitted by the sensory nerves to the brain give rise to sensation, he proceeds:

> And in addition to the different feelings excited in the soul by these different motions of the brain, the animal spirits, without the intervention of the soul, may take their course towards certain muscles, rather than towards others, and thus move the limbs, as I shall prove by an example. If some one moves his hand rapidly towards our eyes, as if he were going to strike us, although we know that he is a friend, that he does it only in jest, and that he will be very careful to do us no harm, nevertheless it will be hard to keep from winking. And this shows, that it is not by the agency of the soul that the eyes shut, since this action is contrary to that volition which is the only, or at least the chief, function of the soul; but it is because the mechanism of our body is so disposed, that the motion of the hand towards our eyes excites another movement in our brain, and this sends the animal spirits into those muscles which cause the eyelids to close.

Since Descartes' time, experiment has eminently enlarged our knowledge of the details of reflex action. The discovery of Bell has enabled us to follow the tracks of the sensory and motor impulses, along distinct bundles of nerve fibres; and the spinal cord, apart from the brain, has been proved to be a great centre of reflex action; but the fundamental conception remains as Descartes left it, and it is one of the pillars of nerve physiology at the present day.

[4.1.5]

V. The motion of any given portion of the matter of the brain excited by the motion of a sensory nerve, leaves behind a readiness to be moved in the same way, in that part. Anything which resuscitates the motion gives rise to the appropriate feeling. This is the physical mechanism of memory.

Descartes imagined that the pineal body (a curious appendage to the upper side of the brain, the function of which, if it have any, is wholly unknown) was the instrument through which the soul received impressions from, and communicated them to, the brain. And he thus endeavours to explain what happens when one tries to recollect something:

> Thus when the soul wills to remember anything, this volition, causing the [pineal] gland to incline itself in different directions, drives the [animal] spirits towards different regions of the brain, until they reach that part in which are the traces, which the object which it desires to remember has left. These traces are produced thus: those pores of the brain through which the [animal] spirits have previously been driven, by reason of the presence of the object, have thereby acquired a tendency to be opened by the animal spirits which return towards them more easily than other pores, so that the animal spirits, impinging on these pores, enter them more readily than others. By this means they excite a particular movement in the pineal gland, which represents the object to the soul, and causes it to know what it is which it desired to recollect.[3]

That memory is dependent upon some condition of the brain is a fact established by many considerations—among the most important of which are the remarkable phenomena of aphasia. And that the condition of the brain on which memory depends, is largely determined by the repeated occurrence of that condition of its molecules, which gives rise to the idea of the thing remembered, is no less certain. Every boy who learns his lesson by repeating it exemplifies the fact. Descartes, as we have seen, supposes that the pores of a given part of the brain are stretched by the animal spirits, on the occurrence of a sensation, and that the part of the brain thus stretched, being imperfectly elastic, does not return to exactly its previous condition, but remains more distensible than it was before. . . .

. . . Physiology is, at present, incompetent to say anything positively about the matter, or to go farther than the expression of the high probability, that every molecular change which gives rise to a state of consciousness, leaves a more or less persistent structural modification, through which the same molecular change may be regenerated by other agencies than the cause which first produced it.

[4.1.6]

Thus far, the propositions respecting the physiology of the nervous system which are stated by Descartes have simply been more clearly defined, more fully illustrated, and, for the most part, demonstrated, by modern physiological research. But there remains a doctrine to which Descartes attached great weight, so that full acceptance of it became a sort of note of a thoroughgoing Cartesian, but which, nevertheless, is so opposed to ordinary prepossessions that it attained more general notoriety, and gave rise to more discussion, than almost any other Cartesian hypothesis. It is the doctrine that brute animals are mere machines or automata, devoid not only of reason, but of any kind of consciousness, which is stated briefly in the "Discourse on Method", and more fully in the "Replies to Four Objections", and in the correspondence with Henry More.

The process of reasoning by which Descartes arrived at this startling conclusion is well shown in the following passage of the "Replies":

> But as regards the souls of beasts, although this is not the place for considering them, and though, without a general exposition of physics, I can say no more on this subject than I have already said in the fifth part of my Treatise on Method; yet, I will further state, here, that it appears to me to be a very remarkable circumstance that no movement can take place, either in the bodies of beasts, or even in our own, if these bodies have not in themselves all the organs and instruments by means of which the very same movements would be accomplished in a machine. So that, even in us, the spirit, or the soul, does not directly move the limbs, but only determines the course of that very subtle liquid which is called the animal spirits, which, running continually from the heart by the brain into the muscles, is the cause of all the movements of our limbs, and often may cause many different motions, one as easily as the other.
>
> And it does not even always exert this determination; for among the movements which take place in us, there are many which do not depend on the mind at all, such as the beating of the heart, the digestion of food, the nutrition, the respiration of those who sleep; and even in those who are awake, walking, singing, and other similar actions, when they are performed without the mind thinking about

them. And, when one who falls from a height throws his hands forward to save his head, it is in virtue of no ratiocination that he performs this action; it does not depend upon his mind, but takes place merely because his senses being affected by the present danger, some change arises in his brain which determines the animal spirits to pass thence into the nerves, in such a manner as is required to produce this motion, in the same way as in a machine, and without the mind being able to hinder it. Now since we observe this in ourselves, why should we be so much astonished if the light reflected from the body of a wolf into the eye of a sheep has the same force to excite in it the motion of flight?

After having observed this, if we wish to learn by reasoning, whether certain movements of beasts are comparable to those which are effected in us by the operation of the mind, or, on the contrary, to those which depend only on the animal spirits and the disposition of the organs, it is necessary to consider the difference between the two, which I have explained in the fifth part of the *Discourse on Method* (for I do not think that any others are discoverable), and then it will easily be seen, that all the actions of beasts are similar only to those which we perform without the help of our minds. For which reason we shall be forced to conclude, that we know of the existence in them of no other principle of motion than the disposition of their organs and the continual affluence of animal spirits produced by the heat of the heart, which attenuates and subtilises the blood; and, at the same time, we shall acknowledge that we have had no reason for assuming any other principle, except that, not having distinguished these two principles of motion, and seeing that the one, which depends only on the animal spirits and the organs, exists in beasts as well as in us, we have hastily concluded that the other, which depends on mind and on thought, was also possessed by them.

Descartes' line of argument is perfectly clear. He starts from reflex action in man, from the unquestionable fact that, in ourselves, co-ordinate, purposive, actions may take place, without the intervention of consciousness or volition, or even contrary to the latter. As actions of a certain degree of complexity are brought about by mere mechanism, why may not actions of still greater complexity be the result of a more refined mechanism? What proof is there that brutes are other than a superior race of marionettes, which eat without pleasure, cry without pain, desire nothing, know nothing, and only simulate intelligence as a bee simulates a mathematician? . . .

[4.1.6]

... Modern research has brought to light a great multitude of facts, which not only show that Descartes' view is defensible, but render it far more defensible than it was in his day. . . .

[4.1.6.1]

... Now if, by some accident, a man's spinal cord is divided, his limbs are paralysed, so far as his volition is concerned, below the point of injury; and he is incapable of experiencing all those states of consciousness which, in his uninjured state, would be excited by irritation of those nerves which come off below the injury. If the spinal cord is divided in the middle of the back, for example, the skin of the feet may be cut, or pinched, or burned, or wetted with vitriol, without any sensation of touch, or of pain, arising in consciousness. So far as the man is concerned, therefore, the part of the central nervous system which lies beyond the injury is cut off from consciousness. It must indeed be admitted, that, if any one think fit to maintain that the spinal cord below the injury is conscious, but that it is cut off from any means of making its consciousness known to the other consciousness in the brain, there is no means of driving him from his position by logic. But assuredly there is no way of proving it . . . [either]. However near the brain the spinal cord is injured, consciousness remains intact, except that the irritation of parts below the injury is no longer represented by sensation. On the other hand, pressure upon the anterior division of the brain, or extensive injuries to it, abolish consciousness. Hence, it is a highly probable conclusion, that consciousness in man depends upon the integrity of the anterior division of the brain, while the middle and hinder divisions of the brain, and the rest of the nervous centres, have nothing to do with it. And it is further highly probable, that what is true for man is true for other vertebrated animals.

We may assume then, that in a living vertebrated animal, any segment of the cerebro-spinal axis (or spinal cord and brain) separated from that anterior division of the brain which is the organ of consciousness, is as completely incapable of giving rise to consciousness as we know it to be incapable of carrying out volitions. Nevertheless, this separated segment of the spinal cord is not passive and inert. On the contrary, it is the seat of extremely remarkable powers. In our imaginary case of injury, the man would, as we have seen, be devoid of sensation in his legs, and would have not the least power of moving them. But, if the soles of his feet were tickled, the legs would be drawn up just as vigorously as they would have been before the injury. We know exactly what happens when the soles of the feet are tickled; a molecular change takes place in the sensory nerves of the skin, and is propagated along them and through the posterior roots of the spinal nerves, which are constituted by them, to the grey matter of the spinal cord. Through that grey matter the molecular motion is reflected into the anterior roots of the same nerves, constituted by the filaments which supply the muscles of the legs, and, travelling along these motor filaments, reaches the muscles, which at once contract, and cause the limbs to be drawn up.

In order to move the legs in this way, a definite co-ordination of muscular contractions is necessary; the muscles must contract in a certain order and with duly proportioned force; and moreover, as the feet are drawn away from the source of irritation, it may be said that the action has a final cause, or is purposive.

Thus it follows, that the grey matter of the segment of the man's spinal cord, though it is devoid of consciousness, nevertheless responds to a simple stimulus by giving rise to a complex set of muscular contractions, co-ordinated towards a definite end, and serving an obvious purpose.

[4.1.6.2.]

If the spinal cord of a frog is cut across, so as to provide us with a segment separated from the brain, we shall have a subject parallel to the injured man, on which experiments can be made without remorse; as we have a right to conclude that a frog's spinal cord is not likely to be conscious, when a man's is not.

Now the frog behaves just as the man did. The legs are utterly paralysed, so far as voluntary movement is concerned; but they are vigorously drawn up to the body when any irritant is applied to the foot. But let us study our frog a little farther. Touch the skin of the side of the body with a little acetic acid, which gives rise to all the signs of great pain in an uninjured frog. In this case, there can be no pain, because the application is made to a part of the skin supplied with nerves which come off from the cord below the point of section; nevertheless, the frog lifts up the limb of the same side, and applies the foot to rub off the acetic acid; and, what is still more remarkable, if the limb be held so that the frog cannot use it, it will, by and by, move the limb of the other side, turn it across the body, and use it for the same rubbing process. It is impossible that the frog, if it were in its entirety and could reason, should perform actions more purposive than these: and yet we have most complete assurance that, in this case, the frog is not acting from purpose, has no consciousness, and is a mere insensible machine.

But now suppose that, instead of making a section of the cord in the middle of the body, it had been made in such a manner as to separate the hindermost division of the brain from the rest of the organ, and suppose the foremost two-thirds of the brain entirely taken away. The frog is then absolutely devoid of any spontaneity; it sits upright in the attitude which a frog habitually assumes; and it will not stir unless it is touched; but it differs from the frog which I have just described in this, that, if it be thrown into the water, it begins to swim, and swims just as well as the perfect frog does. But swimming requires the combination and successive co-ordination of a great number of muscular actions. And we are forced to conclude, that the impression made upon the sensory nerves of the skin of the frog by the contact with the water into which it is thrown, causes the transmission to the central nervous apparatus of an impulse which sets going a certain machinery by which all the muscles of swimming are brought into play in due co-ordination. If the frog be stimulated by some irritating body, it jumps or walks as well as the complete frog can do. The simple sensory impression, acting through the machinery of the cord, gives rise to these complex combined movements.

It is possible to go a step farther. Suppose that only the anterior division of the brain—so much of it as lies in front of the "optic lobes"—is removed. If that operation is performed quickly and skilfully, the frog may be kept in a state of full bodily vigour for months, or it may be for years; but it will sit unmoved. It sees nothing: it hears nothing. It will starve sooner than feed itself, although food put into its mouth is swallowed. On irritation, it jumps or walks; if thrown into the water it swims. If it be put on the hand, it sits there, crouched, perfectly quiet, and would sit there for ever. If the hand be inclined very gently and slowly, so that the frog would naturally tend to slip off, the creature's fore paws are shifted on to the edge of the hand, until he can just prevent himself from falling. If the turning of the hand be slowly continued, he mounts up with great care and deliberation, putting first one leg forward and then another, until he balances himself with perfect precision upon the edge; and if the turning of the hand is continued, he goes through the needful set of muscular operations, until he comes to be seated in security, upon the back of the hand. The doing of all this requires a delicacy of co-ordination, and a precision of adjustment of the muscular apparatus of the body, which are only comparable to those of a rope-dancer. To the ordinary influences of light, the frog, deprived of its cerebral hemispheres, appears to be blind. Nevertheless, if the animal be put upon a table, with a book at some little distance between it and the light, and the skin of the hinder part of its body is then irritated, it will jump forward, avoiding the book by passing to the right or left of it. Therefore, although the frog appears to have no sensation of light, visible objects act through its brain upon the motor mechanism of its body.

[4.1.6.3.]

It is obvious, that had Descartes been acquainted with these remarkable results of modern research, they would have furnished him with far more powerful arguments than he possessed in favour of his view of the automatism of brutes. The habits of a frog, leading its natural life, involve such simple adaptations to surrounding conditions, that the machinery which is competent to do so much without the intervention of consciousness, might well do all. And this argument is vastly strengthened by what has been learned in recent times of the marvellously complex operations which are performed mechanically, and to all appearance without consciousness, by men, when, in consequence of injury or disease, they are reduced to a condition more or less comparable to that of a frog, in which the anterior part of the brain has been removed. A case has recently been published by an eminent French physician, Dr. Mesnet, which illustrates this condition so remarkably, that I make no apology for dwelling upon it at considerable length.[4]

A sergeant of the French army, F_, twenty-seven years of age, was wounded during the battle of Bazeilles, by a ball which fractured his

left parietal bone. He ran his bayonet through the Prussian soldier
who wounded him, but almost immediately his right arm became
paralysed; after walking about two hundred yards, his right leg became similarly affected, and he lost his senses. When he recovered
them, three weeks afterwards, in hospital at Mayence, the right half
of the body was completely paralysed, and remained in this condition for a year. At present, the only trace of the paralysis which remains is a slight weakness of the right half of the body. Three or
four months after the wound was inflicted, periodical disturbances
of the functions of the brain made their appearance, and have continued ever since. The disturbances last from fifteen to thirty hours;
the intervals at which they occur being from fifteen to thirty days.

For four years, therefore, the life of this man has been divided
into alternating phases—short abnormal states intervening between
long normal states.

In the periods of normal life, the ex-sergeant's health is perfect; he
is intelligent and kindly, and performs, satisfactorily, the duties of a
hospital attendant. The commencement of the abnormal state is
ushered in by uneasiness and a sense of weight about the forehead,
which the patient compares to the constriction of a circle of iron;
and, after its termination, he complains, for some hours, of dullness
and heaviness of the head. But the transition from the normal to the
abnormal state takes place in a few minutes, without convulsions or
cries, and without anything to indicate the change to a bystander.
His movements remain free and his expression calm, except for a
contraction of the brow, an incessant movement of the eyeballs, and
a chewing motion of the jaws. The eyes are wide open, and their
pupils dilated. If the man happens to be in a place to which he is accustomed, he walks about as usual; but, if he is in a new place, or if
obstacles are intentionally placed in his way, he stumbles gently
against them, stops, and then, feeling over the objects with his
hands, passes on one side of them. He offers no resistance to any
change of direction which may be impressed upon him, or to the
forcible acceleration or retardation of his movements. He eats,
drinks, smokes, walks about, dresses and undresses himself, rises
and goes to bed at the accustomed hours. Nevertheless, pins may be
run into his body, or strong electric shocks sent through it, without
causing the least indication of pain; no odorous substance, pleasant
or unpleasant, makes the least impression; he eats and drinks with

avidity whatever is offered, and takes asafœtida, or vinegar, or qui-
nine, as readily as water; no noise affects him; and light influences
him only under certain conditions. Dr. Mesnet remarks, that the
sense of touch alone seems to persist, and indeed to be more acute
and delicate than in the normal state: and it is by means of the nerves
of touch, almost exclusively, that his organism is brought into relation with the external world. Here a difficulty arises. It is clear from
the facts detailed, that the nervous apparatus by which, in the normal state, sensations of touch are excited, is that by which external
influences determine the movements of the body, in the abnormal
state. But does the state of consciousness, which we term a tactile
sensation, accompany the operation of this nervous apparatus in the
abnormal state, or is consciousness utterly absent, the man being reduced to an insensible mechanism? . . .

. . . As I have pointed out, it is impossible to prove that F_ is absolutely unconscious in his abnormal state, but it is no less impossible to prove the contrary; and the case of the frog goes a long way to
justify the assumption that, in the abnormal state, the man is a mere
insensible machine.

If such facts as these had come under the knowledge of Descartes,
would they not have formed an apt commentary upon that remarkable passage in the "Treatise on Man", which I have quoted elsewhere, but which is worth repetition:

> All the functions which I have attributed to this machine (the body),
> as the digestion of food, the pulsation of the heart and of the arteries;
> the nutrition and the growth of the limbs; respiration, wakefulness,
> and sleep; the reception of light, sounds, odours, flavours, heat, and
> such like qualities, in the organs of the external senses; the impression
> of the ideas of these in the organ of common sensation and in the
> imagination; the retention or the impression of these ideas on the
> memory; the internal movements of the appetites and the passions;
> and lastly the external movements of all the limbs, which follow so
> aptly, as well the action of the objects which are presented to the
> senses, as the impressions which meet in the memory, that they imitate
> as nearly as possible those of a real man; I desire, I say, that you should
> consider that these functions in the machine naturally proceed from
> the mere arrangement of its organs, neither more nor less than do the
> movements of a clock, or other automaton, from that of its weights
> and its wheels; so that, so far as these are concerned, it is not necessary

to conceive any other vegetative or sensitive soul, nor any other principle of motion or of life, than the blood and the spirits agitated by the fire which burns continually in the heart, and which is no wise essentially different from all the fires which exist in inanimate bodies.

And would Descartes not have been justified in asking why we need deny that animals are machines, when men, in a state of unconsciousness perform, mechanically, actions as complicated and as seemingly rational as those of any animals?

[4.1.7]

But though I do not think that Descartes' hypothesis can be positively refuted, I am not disposed to accept it. The doctrine of continuity is too well established for it to be permissible to me to suppose that any complex natural phenomenon comes into existence suddenly, and without being preceded by simpler modifications; and very strong arguments would be needed to prove that such complex phenomena as those of consciousness, first make their appearance in man. We know, that, in the individual man, consciousness grows from a dim glimmer to its full light, whether we consider the infant advancing in years, or the adult emerging from slumber and swoon. We know, further, that the lower animals possess, though less developed, that part of the brain which we have every reason to believe to be the organ of consciousness in man; and as, in other cases, function and organ are proportional, so we have a right to conclude it is with the brain; and that the brutes, though they may not possess our intensity of consciousness, and though, from the absence of language, they can have no trains of thoughts, but only trains of feelings, yet have a consciousness which, more or less distinctly, foreshadows our own.

I confess that, in view of the struggle for existence which goes on in the animal world, and of the frightful quantity of pain with which it must be accompanied, I should be glad if the probabilities were in favour of Descartes' hypothesis; but, on the other hand, considering the terrible practical consequences to domestic animals which might ensue from any error on our part, it is as well to err on the right side, if we err at all, and deal with them as weaker brethren, who are bound, like the rest of us, to pay their toll for living, and suffer what is needful for the general good. As Hartley finely says, "We seem to be in the place of God to them", and we may justly follow the precedents He sets in nature in our dealings with them.

[4.1.8]

But though we may see reason to disagree with Descartes' hypothesis that brutes are unconscious machines, it does not follow that he was wrong in regarding them as automata. They may be more or less conscious, sensitive, automata; and the view that they are such conscious machines is that which is implicitly, or explicitly, adopted by most persons. When we speak of the actions of the lower animals being guided by instinct and not by reason, what we really mean is that, though they feel as we do, yet their actions are the results of their physical organisation. We believe, in short, that they are machines, one part of which (the nervous system) not only sets the rest in motion, and co-ordinates its movements in relation with changes in surrounding bodies, but is provided with special apparatus, the function of which is the calling into existence of those states of consciousness which are termed sensations, emotions, and ideas. I believe that this generally accepted view is the best expression of the facts at present known.

It is experimentally demonstrable—any one who cares to run a pin into himself may perform a sufficient demonstration of the fact—that a mode of motion of the nervous system is the immediate antecedent of a state of consciousness. All but the adherents of "Occasionalism", or of the doctrine of "Pre-established Harmony" (if any such now exist), must admit that we have as much reason for regarding the mode of motion of the nervous system as the cause of the state of consciousness, as we have for regarding any event as the cause of another. How the one phenomenon causes the other we know, as much or as little, as in any other case of causation; but we have as much right to believe that the sensation is an effect of the molecular change, as we have to believe that motion is an effect of impact; and there is as much propriety in saying that the brain evolves sensation, as there is in saying that an iron rod, when hammered, evolves heat.

As I have endeavoured to show, we are justified in supposing that something analogous to what happens in ourselves takes place in the brutes, and that the affections of their sensory nerves give rise to molecular changes in the brain, which again give rise to, or evolve, the corresponding states of consciousness. Nor can there be any reasonable doubt that the emotions of brutes, and such ideas as they possess, are similarly dependent upon molecular brain changes. Each sensory impression leaves behind a record in the structure of the brain—an "ideagenous" molecule, so to speak, which is competent, under certain conditions, to reproduce, in a fainter condition, the state of consciousness which corresponds with that sensory impression; and it is these "ideagenous molecules" which are the physical basis of memory.

It may be assumed, then, that molecular changes in the brain are the causes of all the states of consciousness of brutes. Is there any evidence that these states of consciousness may, conversely, cause those molecular changes which give rise to muscular motion? I see no such evidence. The frog walks, hops, swims, and goes through his gymnastic performances quite as well without consciousness, and consequently without volition, as with it; and, if a frog, in his natural state, possesses anything corresponding with what we call volition, there is no reason to think that it is anything but a concomitant of the molecular changes in the brain which form part of the series involved in the production of motion.

The consciousness of brutes would appear to be related to the mechanism of their body simply as a collateral product of its working, and to be as completely without any power of modifying that working as the steam-whistle which accompanies the work of a locomotive engine is without influence upon its machinery. Their volition, if they have any, is an emotion indicative of physical changes, not a cause of such changes. . . .

[4.1.9]

. . . Thus far I have strictly confined myself to the problem with which I proposed to deal at starting—the automatism of brutes. . . .

. . . It is quite true that, to the best of my judgment, the argumentation which applies to brutes holds equally good of men; and, therefore, that all states of consciousness in us, as in them, are immediately caused by molecular changes of the brain-substance. It seems to me that in men, as in brutes, there is no proof that any state of consciousness is the cause of change in the motion of the matter of the organism. If these positions are well based, it follows that our mental conditions are simply the symbols in consciousness of the changes which take place automatically in the organism; and that, to take an extreme illustration, the feeling we call volition is not the cause of a voluntary act, but the symbol of that state of the brain which is the immediate cause of that act. We are conscious automata, endowed with free will in the only intelligible sense of that much-abused term—inasmuch as in many respects we are able to do as we like—but none the less parts of the great series of causes and effects which, in unbroken continuity, composes that which is, and has been, and shall be—the sum of existence. . . .

. . . Charles Bonnet, the Genevese naturalist, has embodied the doctrine in language of such precision and simplicity, that I will quote the little known passage of his "Essai de Psychologie" at length:

Another Hypothesis Concerning the Mechanism of Ideas[5]

Philosophers accustomed to judge of things by that which they are in themselves, and not by their relation to received ideas, would not be shocked if they met with the proposition that the soul is a mere spectator of the movements of its body: that the latter performs of itself all that series of actions which constitutes life: that it moves of itself: that it is the body alone which reproduces ideas, compares and arranges them; which forms reasonings, imagines and executes plans of all kinds, etc. This hypothesis, though perhaps of an excessive boldness, nevertheless deserves some consideration.

It is not to be denied that Supreme Power could create an automaton which should exactly imitate all the external and internal actions of man.

I understand by external actions, all those movements which pass under our eyes: I term internal actions, all the motions which in the natural state cannot be observed because they take place in the interior of the body—such as the movements of digestion, circulation, sensation, etc. Moreover, I include in this category the movements which give rise to ideas, whatever be their nature.

In the automaton which we are considering everything would be precisely determined. Everything would occur according to the rules of the most admirable mechanism: one state would succeed another state, one operation would lead to another operation, according to invariable laws; motion would become alternately cause and effect, effect and cause; reaction would answer to action, and reproduction to production.

Constructed with definite relations to the activity of the beings which compose the world, the automaton would receive impressions from it, and, in faithful correspondence thereto, it would execute a corresponding series of motions.

Indifferent towards any determination, it would yield equally to all, if the first impressions did not, so to speak, wind up the machine and decide its operations and its course.

The series of movements which this automaton could execute would distinguish it from all others formed on the same model but which, not having been placed in similar circumstances, would not have experienced the same impressions, or would not have experienced them in the same order.

The senses of the automaton, set in motion by the objects presented to it, would communicate their motion to the brain, the chief motor apparatus of the machine. This would put in action the muscles of the hands and feet, in virtue of their secret connection with the senses. These muscles, alternately contracted and dilated, would approximate or remove the automaton from the objects, in the relation which they would bear to the conservation or the destruction of the machine.

The motions of perception and sensation which the objects would have impressed on the brain, would be preserved in it by the energy of its mechanism. They would become more vivid according to the actual condition of the automaton, considered in itself and relatively to the objects.

Words being only the motions impressed on the organ of hearing and that of voice, the diversity of these movements, their combination, the order in which they would succeed one another, would represent judgments, reasoning, and all the operations of the mind.

A close correspondence between the organs of the senses, either by the opening into one another of their nervous ramifications, or by interposed springs, would establish such a connection in their working, that, on the occasion of the movements impressed on one of these organs, other movements would be excited, or would become more vivid in some of the other senses.

Give the automaton a soul which contemplates its movements, which believes itself to be the author of them, which has different volitions on the occasion of the different movements, and you will on this hypothesis construct a man. . . .

Notes

1. Locke (*Human Understanding*, Book II., chap viii. 37) uses Descartes' illustration for the same purpose, and warns us that "most of the ideas of sensation are no more the likeness of something existing without us than the names that stand for them are the likeness of our ideas, which yet, upon hearing, they are apt to excite in us," a declaration which paved the way for Berkeley.

2. *The Passions of the Soul*, xxxvi.

3. *The Passions of the Soul*, xlii.

4. "De l'Automatisme de la Memoire et du Souvenir, dans le Somnambulisme pathologique." Par le Dr. E. Mesnet, *Journal des Débats*, 7th. August, 1874.

5. *Essai de Psychologie*, chap. xxvii.

INDEX